The DOG LOVERS' Guides

Dachshund

The DOG LOVERS' Guides

Beagle
Boxer
Bulldog
Cavalier King Charles Spaniel
Chihuahua
Cocker Spaniel
Dachshund
French Bulldog
German Shepherd
Golden Retriever
Labrador Retriever
Miniature Schnauzer
Poodle
Pug
Rottweiler
Siberian Husky
Shih Tzu
Yorkshire Terrier

Dachshund

By Jennifer Lowe

Mason Crest
450 Parkway Drive, Suite D
Broomall, PA 19008
www.masoncrest.com

© 2018 by Mason Crest, an imprint of National Highlights, Inc.

Printed and bound in the United States of America.

Series ISBN: 978-1-4222-3848-6
Hardback ISBN: 978-1-4222-3855-4
EBook ISBN: 978-1-4222-7934-2

First printing
1 3 5 7 9 8 6 4 2

Cover photograph by Miguel Rodriguez/Dreamstime.com.

Library of Congress Cataloging-in-Publication Data is on file with the publisher.

QR Codes disclaimer:

You may gain access to certain third-party content ("Third-Party Sites") by scanning and using the QR Codes that appear in this publication (the "QR Codes"). We do not operate or control in any respect any information, products, or services on such Third-Party Sites linked to by us via the QR Codes included in this publication, and we assume no responsibility for any materials you may access using the QR Codes. Your use of the QR Codes may be subject to terms, limitations, or restrictions set forth in the applicable terms of use or otherwise established by the owners of the Third-Party Sites. Our linking to such Third-Party Sites via the QR Codes does not imply an endorsement or sponsorship of such Third-Party Sites, or the information, products, or services offered on or through the Third-Party Sites, nor does it imply an endorsement or sponsorship of this publication by the owners of such Third-Party Sites.

Contents

1 Introducing the Dachshund 6

2 What Should a Dachshund Look Like? 18

3 What Do You Want From Your Dachshund? 28

4 Finding Your Puppy 40

5 A Dachshund-Friendly Home 50

6 Caring for Your Dachshund 74

7 Training Your Dachshund 86

8 Keeping Your Dachshund Busy..................... 102

9 Health Care 108

Find Out More.. 126
Series Glossary of Key Terms........................... 127
Index 128

Key Icons to Look For

 Sidebars: This boxed material within the main text allows readers to build knowledge, gain insights, explore possibilities, and broaden their perspectives by weaving together additional information to provide realistic and holistic perspectives.

 Educational Videos: Readers can view videos by scanning our QR codes, providing them with additional educational content to supplement the text. Examples include news coverage, moments in history, speeches, iconic moments, and much more!

 Series Glossary of Key Terms: This back-of-the-book glossary contains terminology used throughout this series. Words found here increase the reader's ability to read and comprehend higher-level books and articles in this field.

Chapter 1

Introducing the Dachshund

The Dachshund is a breed like no other, with his "wiener dog" conformation and his temperament—a remarkable combination of fearless hunter and faithful companion. Plus, there are two sizes and three coat types to choose from, and a huge variety of colors and patterns.

When you first look at a Dachshund, you might think a dog of this shape and size could never be a working dog. But you would be quite wrong. The Dachshund is designed to go down a hole and dig, and when you look at him, that makes sense. His role was to locate and flush out badgers; as well as needing an outstanding sense of smell to find them, he also needed great courage to dig them out.

Although there are still Dachshunds who track and hunt, the breed has also become one of the most popular companion dogs. The Dachshund is highly adaptable, and his bold, outgoing temperament means he can suit a variety of owners with many different lifestyles.

Physical characteristics

The Dachshund is a small dog, with an elongated body that is close to the ground. He has short legs and big paws. His front legs are particularly powerful, because these were developed for digging. The line of the body ends with a tail that is carried with a slight upward curve—a way for hunters to spot their dogs when they were working in thick undergrowth or were halfway down a hole.

The Dachshund has a most striking head, and he typically carries it in a way that speaks to his boldness and defiance. The strong head is framed by drop ears, while the eyes convey keenness and intelligence.

The Dachshund comes in two sizes: standard and miniature. The varieties are identical in every respect except size—the miniature is simply a smaller, more refined version. In dog shows held under FCI rules (Fédération Cynologique Internationale is the governing body for dog shows in 86 countries around the world, including

Germany), there are three sizes: standard, miniature, and rabbit.

Each size comes in three coat types—smooth, longhaired, or wirehaired—and each variety has its ardent enthusiasts. The smooths look sleek and elegant, the longhairs give a softer and sweeter impression, and the wirehairs, with their bristling eyebrows and beard, look a bit like Civil War generals.

The three coat types and two sizes works out to six varieties. But there are even more choices. There are solid colors, combinations of two colors (solid colors with tan or cream markings), dapples (a merle pattern), brindles (a striped pattern), and sables (red with a dark overlay).

Scenthounds

The Dachshund is a member of the Hound Group in the American Kennel Club (AKC), and is classified as a Scenthound in the United Kennel Club (UKC). Both relate to his hunting ancestry. The Dachshund, along with breeds such as the Basset Hound, the Bloodhound, and the Beagle, hunt by following a scent trail. (Sighthounds, such as Greyhounds, Afghan Hounds, and Salukis, hunt by running down quarry they can see.)

Temperament

The Dachshund has a wonderful temperament; it combines many different facets, but they all add up to make a great companion dog.

The breed standard, which describes the "perfect" Dachshund, gives an excellent account of his character. There are different versions of the standard in different countries and registries, but the Dachshund is variously described as:

- **Smart:** He is quick to size up a situation and can figure things out and use his own initiative.
- **Lively:** He has lots of energy and loves to join in with all activities.
- **Courageous to the point of rashness:** This comes from his hunting ancestry, going underground and confronting a fierce animal such as a badger.
- **Tenacious:** This applies to his tracking skills; once a Dachshund is following a scent, he will be deaf to your calls.
- **Obedient:** With positive training, the Dachshund is ready and willing to cooperate, and can take part in many canine sports.

- **Friendly:** With his outgoing temperament, the Dachshund is ready to greet everyone as his friend.
- **Faithful:** He is a most devoted companion.
- **Versatile:** This is a dog who will adapt to a variety of lifestyles.
- **Passionate:** An unusual adjective to describe a dog, but it sums up the Dachshund's wholehearted attitude to life.
- **Good-tempered:** Every day is a good day for the Dachshund.

Companion dog

The Dachshund is happy in most situations—urban or rural, apartment or ranch, families with children or older owners. His adaptability is his greatest asset. As long as he gets enough exercise and mental stimulation, and is not left on his own for long periods, he will be content.

If you have very small children, it may be better to wait until they are a little older before you get a Dachshund, because he can't withstand a child sitting on his back or really serious roughhousing. But generally the Dachshund will be a lively playmate, as long as mutual respect is established on both sides.

A Dachshund will lead a fulfilling life as a single dog, but he is very sociable and enjoys the company of other dogs. As working dogs, Dachshunds were kept in packs; they have a natural way of relating to their own kind, and can often form strong attachments.

Life expectancy

The Dachshund was developed to be a hardy hunting dog, and if he is bred without exaggeration and given the right care, he will enjoy a good life expectancy. Most dogs reach their early teens, and some do even better. Dachshunds 15 years and older are not unusual. On average, miniatures tend to live a few years longer than standards.

Tracing back in time

Dogs with long bodies and short legs have been bred for centuries. There is even evidence from ancient Egypt of this type of hunting dog. But we need to fast forward to the 18th century to find the origins of the Dachshund that we know today.

The name *Dachshund* means "badger hound" in German—and Germany is the breed's native home. Dogs were needed to work underground to pursue badgers, and so larger hunting dogs and hounds were selectively bred to smaller terriers to produce a small, long-bodied hunter who could give chase through tunnels.

Known as the Dackel or Teckel (a name still used for working dogs), these small dogs hunted by scent, working their way through thick undergrowth to find wild boar and badger. They hunted in packs and were completely fearless; dogs were prepared to dig their way into a badger's den and confront this most formidable of oppo-

nents. The Dachshund's job was to chase the badger from its den and then corner it until the hunters arrived.

Hunters realized that the Dachshund could also be used to hunt rabbits and foxes, if he was small enough to get down the holes leading to the animal's burrow. In the 18th and 19th centuries, the smaller Teckels were selected and crossed with Rat Terriers, Toy Pinschers, and even Chihuahuas to establish a miniature variety. The goal was to keep the tenacity of the large variety, while adding the quickness of the smaller breeds. The result is a small, agile dog who even today excels at field work.

Broadening horizons

The first Dachshunds reached the U.K. in 1840 when Queen Victoria's husband, Prince Albert, received a gift of a number of smooths from Prince Edward of Saxe Weimar. They were kept at Windsor Castle and took part in pheasant shoots. Queen Victoria kept several as pets, and did much to popularize Dachshunds.

Although the breed originated in Germany, the British founded a national Dachshund club in 1881—seven years before its German counterpart. In Britain, they were exhibited at dog shows starting in 1866, where they were called German Badger Dogs. In Germany, however, they remained hunting hounds.

Dachshunds were imported into the United States for several years before they were recognized by the AKC. A black and tan dog named Dash, owned by Dr. G.D. Stewart, in 1885 became the first Dachshund to be registered. The Dachshund Club of America was formed in 1895.

By 1914, the Dachshund was one of the most popular breeds in the United States, and was among the 10 most numerous entries at the Westminster Kennel Club Show. But when the United States entered World War I, the popularity of Dachshunds declined dramatically, because they were used to depict Germany in many wartime propaganda pieces in the United States, Britain, and France. Many Dachshunds were killed; this was probably the low point for the breed.

Developing the varieties

The first of the three coat types to be developed was the smooth, which is said to have a dash of Pinscher. The longhair may have been developed form the smooth just by selective breeding for coat type, or there may be been some spaniel mixed in. The wirehair—the most recent of the three coat types—definitely has some terrier ancestry.

Wirehairs

There is evidence of wirehaired Dachshunds dating back to the 18th century; the wire coat was probably a throwback to the wirehaired Pinschers that were used to develop the breed. However, wirehaired Dachshunds were few in number and did not gain in popularity until the foundation of the German Teckel Klub in Germany in 1888. Soon after, a wirehair named Mordax was exhibited at a show in Berlin and won first prize.

British dealers, who came looking for new stock in Germany, introduced terriers to mate with the smooths. The wirehair gradually became established, and has always been highly valued as a working dog because his tough, wiry coat allows him to work in the thickest undergrowth.

The miniature wirehair was the last of the six varieties to be recognized. They were bred down from standard-size dogs, crossed with miniature smooths.

Longhairs

This variety may have arisen by selectively breeding smooth Dachshunds who had slightly longer coats, but it is more likely that the German Stoberhund, and some of the spaniel breeds, were introduced. Certainly, the early photos of longhairs look very spaniel-like.

In the USA, longhairs were kept mainly as pets, and it was not until 1931 that the first longhaired Dachshund was registered with the AKC.

The miniature variety was developed by breeding longhairs with drop-eared Papillons, known as Phalenes. However, it took many years of dedicated breeding before the miniature longhair achieved the true Dachshund look.

Dachshunds today

Dachshunds are almost always in the AKC top ten most popular breeds, and have been since the 1940s. (World War II did not have the same disastrous effect on the breed as the previous world war.) In 1951 the National Miniature Dachshund Club was formed, and while it has sought to separate the two sizes into different breeds, that has never happened.

The Dachshund's popularity and unique look have made it a favorite of artists, illustrators, toy makers, sculptors, and the advertising business. Dachshund figurines, toys, salt-and-pepper shakers, dishes, and many other breed-related items have been enjoyed since the 19th century.

Dachshunds also enjoyed a period of spectacular popularity among the rich and famous. John Wayne, Clark Gable, Errol Flynn, Carol Lombard, Noel Coward, and Pablo Picasso were among the breed's fans.

Chapter 2

What Should a Dachshund Look Like?

There can be no mistaking a Dachshund, with her long body, short legs, muscular prow of a chest, and a boldly carried head. She is first and foremost a sporting breed, and although the vast majority of Dachshunds are kept as companion dogs, she should still look as if she is ready and able to do a day's work.

The aim of breeders is to produce dogs who are sound, healthy, typical examples of their chosen breed in both looks and temperament. To achieve this, they are guided by a breed standard, which is a written blueprint describing what the perfect Dachshund should look like. In the breed standard, the six Dachshund varieties are treated as one breed, but with specific guidance on size and coat type.

Of course, there is no such thing as a "perfect" dog, but breeders

aspire to produce dogs who conform as closely as possible to the breed standard. In the show ring, it is the dog who comes closest to the standard, in the opinion of the judge, who wins top honors.

This has significance beyond the sport of showing, because the dogs who win in the ring will be used for breeding. The winners of today are therefore responsible for passing on their genes to future generations and preserving the breed in its best form.

General appearance

Long and low to the ground, the Dachshund is short in the leg, but has robust muscular development. The height at the withers (the highest point of the shoulder) should be half the length of the body. Despite her short legs, the Dachshund should be agile and lithe. It is therefore important that she be well balanced and without exaggeration, which could hamper her movement.

The breed standard says, "Appearing neither crippled, awkward, nor cramped in his capacity for movement, the Dachshund is well-balanced with bold and confident head carriage and intelligent, alert facial expression. His hunting spirit, good nose, loud tongue and distinctive build make him well-suited for below-ground work and for beating the bush. His keen nose gives him an advantage over most other breeds for trailing."

Temperament

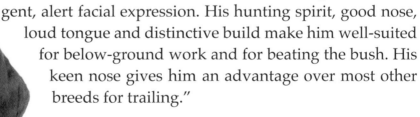

The Dachshund temperament is a wonderful mixture of courageous hunter and good-tempered companion. The standard says, "The Dachshund is clever, lively and courageous

Parts of a Dachshund

Loin · Withers · Topline · Occiput · Stop · Muzzle · Flews · Tail · Shoulder · Chest · Elbow · Foreleg · Wrist · Pastern · Front foot · Hind foot · Thigh · Flank · Dewclaw

to the point of rashness, persevering in above- and below-ground work, with all the senses well-developed. Any display of shyness is a serious fault."

Head and skull

Viewed from above or the side, the head tapers to the tip of the nose and is conical. The skull is slightly arched. (In the wirehaired variety it may be a little broader, although the standard does not specify this.) It slopes gradually, without a prominent stop (the indentation where the muzzle stops and the forehead begins), into a slightly arched muzzle. The standard describes this as a "Roman appearance."

The nose leather is well developed and the nostrils are open, befitting a dog who is bred to be a scenthound.

Eyes

The eyes are almond-shaped and medium in size. They are set obliquely in the skull, and convey a sense of alertness and intelligence. They should be dark, except in chocolates, where they may be lighter. In dapples one or both eyes may be blue, known as "wall" eyes. The bridge bones over the eyes are strongly prominent.

Ears

The ears are set near the top of the head, and they should not be carried too far forward. They should be of moderate length and rounded at the bottom—not narrow or pointy. When a Dachshund is animated, the forward edge of the ears will touch the cheek, framing the face.

Mouth

The lips are described variously as "tightly stretched," covering powerful jaws. The jaws open wide and are hinged well back from the eyes. Bred to be a hunter, the Dachshund must have powerful jaws and well-developed teeth. The correct dentition is a scissors bite, with the teeth on the upper jaw closely overlapping the teeth on the lower jaw.

Neck

The neck is long and muscular, and is crucial in giving the Dachshund her defiant head carriage. It should be slightly arched, running in graceful lines to the shoulders. There should be no evidence of a dewlap (loose skin beneath the lower jaw).

Body

The body is long and muscled. When viewed in profile, the back should lie in the "straightest possible line" between the withers and the short, slightly arched loin (the waist, just behind the ribcage). Although the body must be long, moderation is important; if it is too long the back will be weak and easily injured. Sufficient ground clearance is essential, and a body that hangs loosely between the shoulders is a serious fault.

Forequarters

To work underground, the Dachshund must have powerful forequarters, with long, broad shoulder blades placed obliquely above a robust ribcage. The breastbone is strongly prominent in front. The keel merges gradually into the line of the abdomen and extends well beyond the front legs.

Viewed from the front, the powerful forelegs should fit closely to the forechest, but not so close as to impede movement. They curve slightly inward. The standard says, "The inclined shoulder blades,

Colors and Patterns

Solid: red, chocolate, black, cream

Two colors: black and tan, wild boar (banding on individual hairs), chocolate and tan, gray (blue) and tan, fawn (Isabella) and tan; the markings are over the eyes, sides of the jaw, front, breast, on the paws, around the anus, and under part of the tail.

Dappled: lighter-colored areas contrasting with the darker base color; there may be a large area of white on the chest (double dapples have spots of dapple and spots of white over the entire body; the genes that control this pattern are associated with some serious health problems)

Brindle: black or dark stripes occur over the entire body.

Sable: a uniform dark overlay on red dogs; the overlay hairs are double-pigmented, with the tip of each hair much darker than the base color

Piebald: large patches of a solid color over a white base (this pattern is not recognized by the AKC).

Longhaired red

Smooth dapple

Smooth black and tan

Wirehaired colors (left to right): Chocolate and tan, wild boar, black and tan, gray brindle

upper arms and curved forearms form parentheses that enclose the ribcage."

Again, ground clearance is an important consideration, and it is an area where exaggeration can creep in. At its lowest point between the forelegs, the chest should be halfway between the elbow and the wrist.

Hindquarters

The rear assembly provides the driving force when a Dachshund is moving, and it must be muscular and well put together. The thighs are strong and powerful, and the hind legs should be perfectly parallel. The tail should continue the line of the spine, and be carried up with a slight curve. The tail should not be carried over the back.

Feet

The feet are a Dachshund specialty and seem massive in proportion to the legs. They are designed for digging, with strong well-arched toes that are close together. The nails are strong, and the pads are thick and firm. The back feet are slightly smaller and narrower than the front feet.

Coat

The breed standard describes the three coat types, and the colors, patterns, and physical characteristics of each type. While correct structure is important for every dog, coat color and texture

Dachshund breeds

are less important if you simply want a wonderful pet.

Smooth

This coat is short, dense, and shining. It should not be too long nor too thick. The hair on the underside of the tail may be coarse. The skin should be loose and supple, with little or no wrinkling.

Wirehaired

With the exception of the jaw, eyebrows, and ears, the whole body is covered with a short, thick, hard-textured outer coat, with a finer, softer undercoat. The facial features form distinguished bushy eyebrows and beard; in contrast, the hair on the ears is almost smooth. The legs and feet are neatly furnished with a harsh coat, and the tail is evenly covered with close-fitting hair.

Longhaired

Soft and sleek, the coat may have a slight wave. On the body it should lie flat so as not to obscure the outline, but the hair is longer under the neck, on the forechest, along the undercarriage, and behind the legs. There is long feathering on the ears. The hair is longest on the tail, and, the standards says, "forms a veritable flag."

Size

What size should a Dachshund be? It depends on who you ask! In the USA, Britain, and Canada, there are two sizes, determined by weight at one year and older. The American breed standard stipulates a wide range of 16 to 32 pounds (7 to 14.5 kg) for standards and 11 pounds (about 5 kg) and under for miniatures. The British go for a smaller range of 20 to 26 pounds (9 to 12 kg) for standards and 10 to 11 pounds (4.5 to 5 kg) for miniatures. The Canadians simply say standards are over 11 pounds and the ideal wight for a miniature is 10 pounds.

In countries governed by the FCI, the three sizes are determined by chest circumference at 15 months and older. This dates back to the Dachshund's working ancestry, where the circumference of the chest determined what size hole the Dachshund could go down. The standard has a chest circumference of 35 cm (13.8 inches) or more, and the maximum weight is 9 kg (just under 20 pounds). The miniature has a chest circumference of from 30 cm (about 12 inches) to 35 cm. The rabbit Dachshund has a chest circumference of up to 30 cm.

Gait/movement

The Dachshund "must have agility, freedom of movement, and endurance to do the work for which he was developed," the standard says. The front legs should reach forward without too much lift, and operate in unison with the driving action of the hind legs. Viewed from the front, the legs do not move in exact parallel planes, but incline slightly inward. However, the feet must travel parallel to the line of motion. Overall, she should move with a smooth and fluid stride, covering the ground with ease.

Chapter 3

What Do You Want From Your Dachshund?

There are hundreds of dog breeds to choose from, so how can you be sure the Dachshund is the right breed for you? Before you take the plunge into Dachshund ownership, weigh the pros and cons so you can be 100 percent confident that this breed is best suited to your lifestyle.

Companion

The Dachshund originally comes from working stock but, for most dogs, this part of his history is firmly in the past and it is in the role of companion that the Dachshund excels. He is a natural fit in a family, and he thrives on being part of a busy household. He takes a keen interest in everything that is going on, and will be the self-

appointed guard of your home. In fact, the Dachshund is very friendly and welcomes visitors, but he likes to give warning. A Dachshund's bark is deep and sonorous, and gives the impression of a far bigger dog.

The description of the Dachshund temperament in the breed standard applies to all varieties. However, owners agree that there are some minor differences, and these may influence your choice. The consensus is that standard wirehairs are the most active and extroverted, standard longhairs are the most laid-back, and standard smooths are more "one person" or "one family" dogs. Miniatures are sweet-natured, need less exercise, and are ideally suited to owners with less active lifestyles.

There is one more point to consider: The Dachshund bonds closely with his family, and this is particularly true of miniatures,

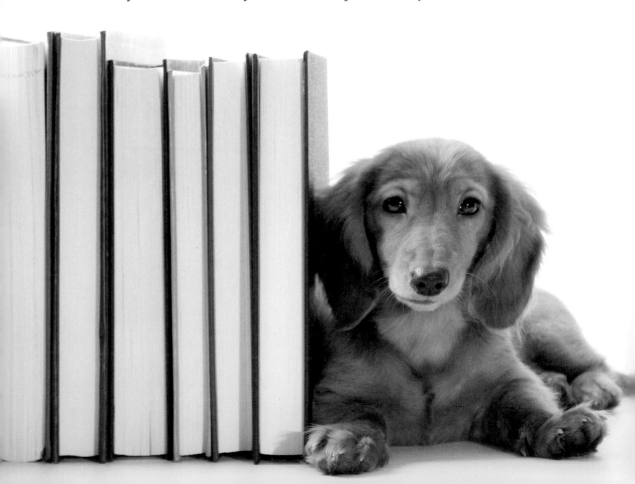

but you do not want your Dachshund to become too dependent. If your dog has not learned how to spend some time alone, he may become anxious and feel that he has been deserted. This is distressing for both dog and owner, and can reach a point where a dog barks constantly when he is left alone. Behaviorists call this "separation anxiety." To prevent this, accustom your puppy to spending short periods on his own—ideally when  he is safe and secure in an indoor crate—and he will understand that although you go away, you always come back.

Show dog

Do you hope to exhibit your Dachshund in the show ring? This is a demanding sport and often becomes highly addictive, but you must have the right dog to start with.

If you plan to show your Dachshund, you need to track down a show quality puppy, and train him so he will perform in the show ring, stand patiently on a judging table, and accept the detailed hands-on examination he will be subjected to.

Show presentation is very important, and the time and expertise required depends on the dog's coat type. Smooths are the most straightforward, longhairs need extensive grooming, and wirehairs are high maintenance; the choice is yours.

It is also important to bear in mind that not every puppy with show potential develops into a top-quality show dog, so you must be prepared to love your Dachshund and give him a home for life, even if he doesn't make the grade.

Working dog

The Dachshund's original role of hunting badger and wild boar is now history, but there are working dogs, known as Teckels, who work for a living. Their role is to keep down vermin, and they also perform the very useful task of tracking fallen deer. If you are interested in this aspect of Dachshund ownership, you will need to go to a breeder who specializes in working lines.

Sports dog

The intelligent Dachshund is more than capable of advanced training, and will enjoy the challenge of many of the canine sports. Obviously, you need to find a sport that suits his conformation (see chapter 8 for more on this topic), but the Dachshund is very versatile, and with positive training, he will always be prepared to have a go.

What does your Dachshund want from you?

A dog cannot speak for himself, so we need to view the world from a canine perspective and figure out what a Dachshund needs to live a happy, contented, and fulfilling life.

Time and commitment

First of all, a Dachshund needs a commitment that you will care for him all his life—guiding him through his puppyhood, enjoying his adulthood, and being there for him in his later years. If all dog owners were prepared to make this pledge, there would hardly be any homeless dogs.

The Dachshund's primary role is to be a companion, and this is what he must be for you. If you cannot give your Dachshund the time and commitment he deserves, it's best to put off owning a dog until your circumstances change.

Practical matters

The Dachshund is an adaptable dog and will cope with varying amounts of exercise. However, standards need considerably more exercise than miniatures. A standard has the energy and endurance to enjoy long walks, but he will cope with shorter outings, particularly if there is an element of variety. Miniatures may not require so much exercise, but their needs should not be neglected. A miniature is still a hound at heart and will relish the opportunity to use his nose and explore new places.

When it comes to grooming, you need to choose your variety with care, as the workload varies greatly: smooth (minimal), longhair (medium care), wirehair (probably needs a professional groomer).

Mental stimulation

The mistake many owners make is thinking that a small dog does not need to be trained. This is a disaster with almost any breed, but particularly so with the Dachshund, who is a hound—bred to use his brain and to take the initiative. Hounds have a reputation for being single-minded and even a bit stubborn.

A well-trained Dachshund is a joy to own, but you cannot leave this highly intelligent dog to his own devices. Although he doesn't have an ounce of malice in his make-up, a Dachshund who is allowed to live without any rules is not fun to live with. He will become very demanding—and if he doesn't get what he wants, he may bark at you until you give in.

As a responsible owner, you must give your dog some training, so he is well-mannered and cooperative. You must channel his energy and his intelligence. It does not matter what you do with him—training exercises, teaching tricks, trips out in the car, or going for new, interesting walks. All are equally appreciated, and will give your Dachshund a purpose in life.

Things to think about

Now that you have decided a Dachshund is the dog for you, and you have figured out whether you want a standard or a miniature, you can narrow your choice still further so you know exactly what kind of dog you are looking for. Do remember, though, that health and temperament are the most important considerations when

choosing a dog. Things like color and pattern and even gender are secondary.

Color and Pattern

There is a brilliant array of colors and patterns to choose from, and all Dachshund enthusiasts have their favorites. Generally, the choice is narrower in wirehairs, with wild boar, chocolate, and red being most readily available.

Take great care if your preference is for a dapple Dachshund. The pattern is very attractive, but you will need to do some extra research on the breeding stock. Puppies born from mating dapple to dapple—known as double dapples—have a high risk of developing conditions such as congenital deafness and blindness.

Choosing a puppy

Male or female?

Male or female really does come down to personal preference. In some breeds males are a bit larger, but in Dachshunds the only real size difference is whether you choose a standard or a miniature.

Some owners think females are more loving and affectionate, but owners of males would swear the opposite! They would claim that males may be more independent but they are also more loyal. The only certainty is that all dogs are individuals, and you can never second-guess how your Dachshund is going to turn out.

You may find a female slightly more difficult to care for, as you will need to cope with her seasonal cycle, which will start around six to nine months of age, with fertile seasons occurring every six months or so thereafter. During the three-week period of a season, you will need to keep your female away from males who have not been neutered to eliminate the risk of an unwanted pregnancy. Some owners report that their female Dachshunds become a little moody or withdrawn in the time leading up to, and during, a season.

Spaying puts an end to the seasons, and also has many attendant health benefits. The operation is usually carried out at about six months of age. Ask your veterinarian for more information.

An intact male may not cause many problems, although some do have a stronger tendency to urine mark, which could include inside the house. However, training will usually put a stop to this. An intact

Rescued Dogs

We are fortunate that very few Dachshunds end up with rescue groups, and this is often through no fault of the dog. The reasons are various, ranging from illness or death of the original owner to family breakdown, changing jobs, or even the arrival of a new baby.

It is unlikely that you will find a Dachshund in a shelter or from an all-breed rescue group. But many Dachshund breed clubs run rescue groups, and this will be your best option if you want to adopt a rescued Dachshund.

Try to find out as much as you can about the dog's history, so you know exactly what you are taking on. You need to be realistic about what you are capable of achieving, so you can be sure you can give the dog you are considering a permanent home.

You need to give a rescued Dachshund plenty of time and patience as he settles into his new home, but if all goes well, you will have the reward of knowing that you have given your dog a second chance at a happy life.

male will also be on the lookout for females in season, and this may lead to difficulties, depending on your circumstances.

Neutering (castrating) a male is a relatively simple operation, and there are associated health benefits. Again, you should seek advice from your veterinarian.

More than one?

Dachshunds are sociable dogs and certainly enjoy one another's company. But you would be wise to guard against the temptation of getting two puppies of similar ages, or two from the same litter.

Unfortunately, there are some unscrupulous breeders who en-

courage people to do this, but they are thinking purely in terms of profit and not considering the welfare of the puppies.

Looking after one puppy is hard work, but taking on two pups at the same time is more than double the workload. Housetraining is a nightmare, and often you don't even know which puppy is making mistakes. Training is impossible unless you separate the two puppies and give them each one-on-one attention.

The puppies will never be bored, as they have each other to play with. However, the likelihood is that the pair will form a close bond, and you will come in a poor second.

If you do decide to add to your Dachshund population, wait at least 12 to 18 months, until your first dog is fully trained and settled, and is more grown-up, before taking on a puppy. The best advice is to get dogs of opposite sexes. Although this means you will definitely need to neuter one or both dogs, the male-female relationship seems to work best.

An adult dog

You may decide to miss out on the puppy phase and start with an adult dog instead. It may be harder to find one, but it's not impossible. Sometimes a breeder may have a young adult they kept on in the hopes he would turn out to be a show dog, but some minor flaw means he is not suitable for showing but is perfect for a family pet. In some cases, a breeder may rehome a female when her breeding career is at an end, so she will enjoy the benefits of getting more individual attention. And of course, there are always Dachshunds from rescue groups.

There are advantages to taking on an adult dog, as you know exactly what you are getting. The upheaval of changing homes can be quite upsetting, though, so you will need to have plenty of patience during the settling-in period.

Chapter 4

Finding Your Puppy

Your aim is to find a healthy puppy who is typical of the breed and has been reared with the greatest possible care. Where do you start?

A great way to find a puppy is to attend a dog show where Dachshunds are being shown. You'll have a chance to see Dachshunds of all varieties.

At first, the dogs of each variety look very similar, although you will see different colors. But when you look carefully, you will see subtle differences. This is because breeders produce dogs with a family likeness, and seeing a number of dogs in the ring will give you the opportunity to decide that type you prefer.

When judging is finished, talk to the exhibitors and find out more about their dogs. They may not have puppies available, but some will be planning a litter, and you may decide to put your name on a waiting list.

Internet research

The Internet is an excellent resource, but when it comes to finding a puppy, use it with care.

Do go to the websites of the big registries. The American Kennel Club (AKC) and the United Kennel Club (UKC) both have excellent websites that will give you information about the Dachshund as a breed and what to look for when choosing a puppy. You will also find contact details for local and national breed clubs.

Both sites have lists of breeders who may have puppies available, and you can look out for breeders of merit on the AKC site, which means a code of conduct has been adhered to.

Do go to the sites of Dachshund breed clubs. On breed club websites you will find lots of useful information that will help you care for your Dachshund. There may be contact details for breeders in your area, or you may need to go through the club secretary. Some websites also have a list of breeders who have puppies available. The advantage of going through a breed club is that members will follow a code of ethics, and this will give you some guarantees regarding breeding stock and health checks.

Do not look at puppies for sale online. There are legitimate Dachshund breeders with their own websites, and they may occasionally ad-

vertise a litter, although in most cases reputable breeders have waiting lists for their puppies.

The danger comes from unscrupulous breeders who produce puppies purely for profit, with no thought for the health of the dogs they breed and no care given to rearing the litter. Photos of puppies are hard to resist, but never make a decision based purely on an advertisement. You need to find out who the breeder is, visit their premises, and meet the litter before making a decision.

Responsible breeders

Responsible breeders raise their puppies at home and underfoot. They have one or, at the most, two litters at a time. They carefully study the pedigrees of the male and female before they arrange any breeding, with an eye toward breeding the healthiest, most temperamentally sound dogs. Responsible breeders belong to a breed club and are involved in their breed.

Responsible breeders register their puppies with the AKC or the UKC. (Registration with a well-established kennel club is a guarantee that your Dachshund is truly a Dachshund, but it is not a guarantee of good health or temperament.) They are able to hand over registration documents at the time of sale. Their breeding dogs are permanently identified by microchip or DNA. They screen them for hereditary health problems, and can tell you exactly which screening tests their dogs have had and what the results were.

Responsible breeders socialize all their puppies in a home environment. They provide written advice on feeding, ongoing training, socialization, parasite control, and vaccinations. They are available

for phone calls after you buy their puppies, and will take a dog back at any time. They have a written contract of sale for each puppy that conforms to your state's laws.

Questions, questions, questions

When you find a breeder with puppies available, you should have lots of questions, including:

- Where have the puppies been reared? (A home environment gives them the best possible start in life.)
- How many are in the litter? What colors are they? How many of each sex?
- How many have already been spoken for? (The breeder will probably be keeping a puppy to show or for breeding, and there may be a number of potential buyers on a waiting list.)
- Can I see the mother with her puppies? (The answer should always be yes. Everything should look and smell clean and healthy. The mother should be a well-socialized dog. She may be a little protective of her babies, but she should act like a typical Dachshund.)
- What age are the puppies?
- When will they be ready to go to their new homes?

Bear in mind puppies need to be with their mother and siblings until they are at least 10 weeks of age. Otherwise they miss out on vital learning and communication skills, and this will have a detrimental effect on them for the rest of their lives.

You should also be prepared to answer a number of searching questions so the breeder can check if you are suitable as a potential owner of one of their precious puppies. Don't be offended! They take seriously their responsibility for every puppy they produce, and that's a good thing. You may be asked:

- How big is your home? Does it have a yard?
- Do you have children/grandchildren? What are their ages?

- Is someone at home the majority of the time?
- What is your previous experience with dogs?
- Have you considered the costs of dog ownership, including coat care?
- Do you have plans to show your Dachshund?

The breeder is not being intrusive; they need to understand the type of home you will be able to provide, so they can match you with the right dog.

Be very wary of a breeder who does not ask you questions. They may be more interested in making money from the puppies rather than ensuring that they go to good homes. They may also have taken other short cuts that may prove disastrous in terms of vet bills and heartache.

Health issues

In common with all purebred dogs, the Dachshund suffers from a few hereditary problems. The most significant one affects the back, but most hereditary conditions relate to the eyes. To try to eliminate these health problems from the breed, an annual eye examination

should be considered essential for breeding animals. (Learn more about hereditary health problems in chapter 9.)

Puppy watching

All puppies are irresistible. When you look at a litter you will be entranced; each pup seems to have her own very individual character. But this is a situation where you must not let your heart rule your head. You are making a long-term commitment, so you need to be 100 percent sure that the parents are healthy and the puppies have been reared with love and care.

It is a good idea to have a mental checklist of what to look out for when you visit a breeder. You want to see:

- A clean, hygienic environment.
- Puppies who are outgoing and friendly, and eager to meet you.
- A sweet-natured mother who is ready to show off her babies.
- Puppies who are well-fleshed-out but not pot-bellied, which could be an indication of worms.
- Coats that are look clean and healthy, with no sign of scaly or sore patches.
- Bright eyes, with no sign of soreness or discharge.
- Clean ears that smell fresh.
- No discharge from the nose.
- Clean rear ends—matting could indicate upset tummies.

- Lively pups who are keen to play.

It is important to see the mother with her puppies; this will give you a good idea of the temperament they are likely to inherit. It is also helpful if you can meet other close relatives so you can see the type of Dachshunds the breeder produces.

In most cases, you will not be able to see the father (sire), as most breeders will travel some distance to find a stud dog who is not too close to their own bloodlines and complements their bitch. However, you should be able to see photos of him and be able to examine his pedigree and show record.

Companion puppy

If you are looking for a Dachshund as a companion, you should be guided by the breeder, who will have spent hours and hours puppy watching, and will know each of the pups as individuals. It is tempting to choose a puppy yourself, but the breeder will take into account your family, your home, and your lifestyle, and will help you to pick the most suitable puppy.

By all means, get a pup of the size and coat type you like best, but remember that color and pattern are really not important.

Show puppy

If you are buying a puppy with the hope of showing her, make sure you make this clear to the breeder. A lot of planning goes into producing a litter, and although all the puppies will have been reared with equal care, there will be one or two who have show potential.

Ideally, recruit a breed expert to inspect the puppies with you, so you have the benefit of an objective evaluation. The breeder will also help with your choice, as they will want to ensure that only their best dogs are exhibited in the show ring. Look for:

- A head with the correct conical shape. The eyes should be almond-shaped and dark. They may be lighter in chocolate Dachshunds, and in dapples one or both eyes may be blue.
- The body should be that of an adult in miniature, with a level topline and a tail that follows the line of the back.
- The forechest is visible but not fully developed.
- Good angulation front and rear gives a balanced appearance.
- The correct scissors bite. The bite can change as a puppy develops, so this can only be a guideline.
- An extroverted, outgoing temperament.

Coats are hard to assess at this stage, as all Dachshund puppies are born with smooth coats. In longhairs the feathering appears gradually; longhaired pups who look almost smooth until late in puppyhood seem to develop the best coats.

Wirehairs will show a trace of beard, and they will have some longer, coarser hairs on the body, legs, and in between the toes. There are two types of wire coat: the classic wire and the pin wire which, at this stage, looks completely smooth. When the adult coat comes in on a pin wire, the facial furnishings are minimal. The advantage of this coat is that it may require less grooming.

Remember, there are no guarantees. If your Dachshund fails to make the grade in the show ring, she will still be an outstanding companion and a much-loved member of your family.

Chapter 5

A Dachshund-Friendly Home

I t may seem like forever before your Dachshund puppy is ready to leave the breeder and come home with you. But you can fill the time by getting your home ready, and buying the equipment you will need.

In the home

The Dachshund is a great explorer and will be on the lookout for anything that seems new and interesting. If you add in a puppy's natural curiosity, you will see that your house is the equivalent of one big playground. Of course, you want your puppy to have fun, but the top priority is to keep him safe.

The best plan is to decide which rooms your Dachshund will have access to, and make these areas puppy friendly. Trailing electrical cords are a major hazard, and these will need to be secured out of reach. You will need to make sure all cupboards and cabinets are secure, particularly in the kitchen and bathroom, where you may store

cleaning materials that could be toxic to dogs. Household plants can also be poisonous, so these will need to relocated, along with breakable ornaments.

The Dachshund's elongated body means that he is vulnerable while he is growing, so you will need to prevent him from bounding up and down the stairs. The best way of doing this is to use a baby gate—making sure your puppy cannot squeeze through the sides, which could result in injury.

In the yard

The Dachshund will not leap over fences—but he will dig under them. This means that he can find his way out very easily if there are gaps under the fence or if he burrows under bushes. You therefore need to inspect all boundaries for possible escape routes. Also check the gates leading from the yard to ensure they close and fasten securely.

If you are an avid gardener, you may want to protect your prized plants from unwanted attention. Some dog owners allocate a specific area of the yard as a digging patch, which keeps everyone happy.

Find out if your garden contains plants that are poisonous to dogs. There is not enough room to list them all here, but you can find a full list at www.aspca.org/pet-care/animal-poison-control/toxic-and-non-toxic-plants.

You will also need to designate a toileting area. This will assist in the housetraining process, and it will also make cleaning up easier.

House rules

Before your puppy comes home, hold a family conference to decide on the house rules. For example, is your Dachshund going to be allowed to roam the house freely, or will you keep him in the kitchen unless you can supervise him elsewhere? When you are on the sofa, is he allowed to come up on your lap for a cuddle?

These are personal choices, but once you have allowed your puppy to do something, he will think it is always allowed, regardless of whether you change your mind. You and your family must make decisions and stick with them. Otherwise your puppy will be upset and confused, not understanding what you want of him.

A Dachshund should not be allowed to jump on and off furniture, which could be harmful to his back. If are going to allow your

Dachshund on the sofa or the armchair, you must be there to help him on and off, or get some doggy steps or ramps for him.

Shopping for your Dachshund

There are some essential items you will need for your Dachshund. It's best to buy what you need before you bring your dog home. You'll have enough to do with a new dog in the house! If you choose wisely, much of it will last for many years to come.

Indoor crate

Rearing a puppy is so much easier if you invest in an indoor crate. It provides a safe haven for your puppy at night, when you have to go out during the day, and at other times when you cannot supervise him. A puppy needs a base where he feels safe and secure, and where he can rest undisturbed. An indoor crate is the perfect den, and many adult dogs continue to use them throughout their lives. It is therefore important to buy a crate that is large enough for your Dachshund when he is fully grown.

Think about where you are going to put the crate. The kitchen is usually the most suitable place, as this is the hub of family life. Try to find a snug corner where the puppy can rest when he wants to, but where he can also see what is going on around him and still be with the family.

Beds and bedding

The crate will need to be lined with bedding, and the best type to buy is synthetic fleece. This is warm and cozy, and as moisture soaks through it, your puppy will not have a wet bed when he is tiny and is still unable to go through the night without relieving himself. This type of bedding is machine washable and easy to dry. Buy two pieces, so you have one to use while the other piece is in the wash.

If you have purchased a crate, you may not feel the need to

buy an extra bed, although many Dachshunds like to have a bed in the family room so they feel part of household activities. There is an amazing array of dog beds to chose from—couches, bean bags, cushions, baskets, igloos, mini-four posters—so you can take your pick! Before you make a major investment, wait until your puppy has gone through the chewing phase; you will be surprised at how much damage can be inflicted by small teeth.

Collar and leash

You may think it's not worth buying a collar for the first few weeks, but the sooner your pup gets used to it, the better. All you need is a lightweight nylon puppy collar; you can buy something more fancy when your Dachshund is fully grown.

A nylon leash is suitable for early leash training, but make sure

the fastening is secure. Again, you can invest in a more expensive leash at a later date—there are lots of attractive collar and leash sets to choose from.

ID

Your Dachshund needs to wear some form of ID when he is out and about. This can be in the form of a tag engraved with your contact details attached to the collar. When your Dachshund is full-grown, you can buy an embroidered collar with your contact details, which eliminates the danger of the tag becoming detached from the collar.

You may also wish to consider a permanent form of ID. Increasingly breeders get puppies microchipped before they go to their new homes. A microchip is the size of a grain of rice. It is injected by a vet under the dog's skin, usually between the shoulder blades, with a special needle.

Each chip has its own unique identification number, which can only be read by a special scanner. That ID number is then registered on a national database with your name and contact details, so that if your dog is lost, he can be taken to any vet or rescue center, where he is scanned and then you are contacted.

Bowls

Your Dachshund will need two bowls—one for food, and one for fresh drinking water, which should always be available. A stainless steel bowl is a good choice for food, as it is tough and hygienic. Plastic bowls may be chewed, and there is a danger that bacteria can collect in the small cracks that appear over time.

You can buy a second stainless steel bowl for drinking water, or you may prefer a heavier ceramic bowl that will not be knocked over so easily.

Food

The breeder will let you know what your puppy is eating

Feeding puppies

and should provide a full diet sheet to guide you through the first six months of your puppy's feeding schedule. Make sure you know how much he is eating per meal, how many meals per day, when to increase the amounts given per meal, and when to decrease the meals per day.

The breeder should provide you with some food when you go pick up your puppy, but it is worth making inquiries in advance about the availability of the brand that is recommended.

Grooming equipment

What you need will depend on your Dachshund's coat. All that is needed for the smooth is a hound glove, which has the curved wire bristles of a slicker brush embedded into a glove or mitt. Both longhairs and wirehairs need a good-quality bristle brush and a wide-toothed steel comb for the longer hair and feathering. A slicker brush is useful for getting out mats and tangles from longhaired Dachshunds.

In addition, you should buy nail clippers, a toothbrush, and toothpaste that is specially formulated for dogs.

Toys

The Dachshund can be surprisingly destructive, so soft, squeaky toys are best avoided. The more robust toys, such as tug toys, and hard rubber items, are ideal. A hollow hard rubber toy can also be stuffed with food, and this will give your Dachshund something to do when he has to be left on his own.

It is important to get into the habit of checking toys regularly for signs of wear and tear. If your puppy swallows a chunk of rubber or plastic, it could cause an internal blockage. This could involve costly surgery to remove the offending item, or at worst, it could prove fatal.

Finding a veterinarian

Do this before you bring your dog home, so you have a vet to call if there is a problem. Speak to other pet owners you might know, to see who they recommend. It is as important to find a good vet as it is to find a good doctor for yourself. You need to find someone you can build up a good rapport with and have complete faith in. Word of mouth is really the best recommendation.

When you contact a veterinary practice, ask what the arrangements are for emergency and after-hours coverage. Do any of the vets in the practice have experience treating Dachshunds? What facilities are available at the practice?

If you are satisfied with what your find, and the staff appear to be helpful and friendly, book an appointment so your puppy can have a health check a couple of days after you bring him home.

Settling in

When you first arrive home with your puppy, be careful not to overwhelm him. You and your family are hugely excited, but the puppy is in a completely strange environment with new sounds, smells, and sights. This is a daunting experience, even for the boldest of pups!

The majority of Dachshund puppies are very confident: exploring their new surroundings, wanting to play right away, and quickly making friends. Others need a little longer to settle in. Keep a close check on your puppy's body language and reactions so you can proceed at a pace he is comfortable with.

First, let him explore the yard. He will probably need to relieve himself after the journey home, so take him to the toileting area you have designated, and, when he performs, give him plenty of praise.

When you take your puppy indoors, let him investigate again. Show him his crate and encourage him to go in by throwing in a

treat. Let him have a sniff, and allow him to go in and out as he wants to. Later on, when he is tired, you can put him in the crate while you stay in the room. In this way, he will learn to settle and will not think he is being abandoned.

It is a good idea to feed your puppy in his crate, at least to begin with, as this helps to build up a positive association. It will not be long

before your Dachshund sees his crate as his own special den and will go there as a matter of choice. Some owners place a blanket over the crate, covering the back and sides, so that it is even more cozy and den-like.

Meeting the family

Resist the temptation to invite friends and neighbors to come and meet the new arrival. Your puppy needs to focus on getting to know his new family for the first few days. Try not to swamp your Dachshund with too much attention; there will be plenty of time for cuddles later on!

If you have children, you need to keep everything as calm as possible. Your puppy may not have met children before, and even if he has, he will still find them strange and unpredictable. A puppy can easily become alarmed by too much noise, or he may go to the opposite extreme and become over-excited, which can lead to mouthing and nipping.

The best plan is to get the children to sit on the floor and give them all a treat. Each child can then call the puppy, pet him, and offer a treat. In this way the puppy is making the decisions rather than being forced into interactions he may find stressful.

If he tries to nip or mouth, make sure there is a toy handy, so his attention can be diverted to something he is allowed to bite. If you do this consistently, he will learn to inhibit his desire to mouth when he is interacting with people.

Right from the start, impose a rule that the children are not allowed to pick up or carry the puppy. They can cuddle him when they are sitting on the floor. This may sound a little severe, but a wriggly puppy can be dropped in an instant, sometimes with disastrous consequences.

Involve all family members with the day-to-day care of your puppy. This will enable the bond to develop with the whole family as opposed to just one person. Encourage the children to train and reward the puppy.

The animal family

Dachshunds are sociable and enjoy the company of other dogs. But make sure you supervise early interactions so relations with the resident dog get off to a good start.

Your adult dog may be allowed to meet the puppy at the breeder's, which is ideal because the older dog will not feel threatened if he is away from home. But if this is not possible, allow your dog to smell the puppy's bedding (bedding supplied by the breeder is fine) before they actually meet, so he can familiarize himself with the puppy's scent.

Outdoors is the best place for introducing the puppy, because the adult dog will regard it as neutral territory. She will probably take a great interest in the puppy and sniff him all over. Most puppies are naturally submissive in this situation, and your pup may lick the other dog's mouth or roll over on his back. Try not to interfere, as this is the natural way dogs get to know each other. You will only need to intervene if the older dog is too boisterous, and alarms the puppy. In this case, it is a good idea to put the adult on her leash so you have some measure of control.

It rarely takes long for an adult dog to accept a puppy, particularly if you make a big fuss over the older dog so that she still feels spe-

cial. However, do not take any risks and supervise all interactions for the first few weeks. If you need to leave the dogs alone, always make sure your puppy is safe in his crate.

Meeting a cat should be supervised in a similar way, but do not allow your puppy to be rough, because the cat may retaliate using her sharp claws. A Dachshund puppy may get over-excited by the sight of a new furry friend, and may try to chase the cat. Make sure you stop this immediately, before bad habits develop. The best way to do this is to keep distracting your puppy by calling him to you and offering him treats. This way, he will switch his focus from the cat to you, and you can reward him for his good behavior.

Generally, the canine-feline relationship should not cause any serious problems. Indeed, many Dachshunds count the family cat among their best friends. The key to success here is to make sure the cat has plenty of elevated spots all over the house, where she can get away from the dog.

Feeding

The breeder will generally provide enough food for the first few days, so the puppy does not have to cope with a change in diet—and possible digestive upset—along with all the stress of a new home.

Some puppies polish off their food from the first meal; others are more concerned about their new surroundings and are too distracted to eat.

Do not worry if your puppy seems disinterested in his food for the first day or so. Give him 10 minutes to eat what he wants and then remove the leftovers and start fresh at the next meal.

Do not make the mistake of trying to tempt his appetite with tasty treats, or you will end up with a picky eater. Obviously, if you have any concerns about your puppy in the first few days, seek advice from your veterinarian.

The first night

Your puppy will have spent the first weeks of his life with his mother, or curled up with his siblings. He is then taken from everything he knows as familiar, lavished with attention by his new family—and then comes bed time when he is left all alone. It is little wonder that he feels abandoned.

The best plan is to establish a nighttime routine, and then stick to it so that your puppy knows what is happening and what is expected of him. Take your puppy outside to relieve himself, and then settle him in his crate.

Some people leave a low light on for the puppy at night for the first week, others have tried a radio as company or a ticking clock. A covered hot-water bottle, filled with warm water, can also be a comfort. Like people, puppies are individuals and what works for one

does not necessarily work for another. It can be trial and error.

Be very positive when you leave your puppy on his own. Do not linger, or keep returning; this will only make the situation more difficult. It is inevitable that he will protest to begin with, but if you stick to your routine, he will accept that he gets left at night—but you always return in the morning.

Rescued dogs

Settling an older, rescued dog in your home is very similar to a puppy. You will need to do the same shopping and make the same preparations for his homecoming. As with a puppy, an adult dog will need you to be consistent, so start as you mean to go on.

There is often an initial honeymoon period when you bring a rescued dog home, and he will be on his best behavior for the first few weeks. It is after this that the true nature of the dog will show, so be prepared for subtle changes in his behavior. It may be advisable to register with a reputable training club, so you can seek advice on any training or behavior issues at an early stage.

Above all, remember that a rescued dog ceases to be a rescued dog the moment he enters his forever home with you, and should be treated like any other family pet.

Housetraining

This is an aspect of training that most first-time puppy owners dread, but it should not be a problem as long as you are prepared to put in the time and effort.

Some breeders start the housetraining process by providing the litter with paper or training pads, so they learn to keep their sleeping quarters clean. This is a step in the right direction, but most pet owners want their puppies to toilet outside.

You will have already allocated a toileting area in your yard or elsewhere outside when preparing for your puppy's homecoming. You need to take your puppy to this area every time he needs to relieve himself, so he builds up an association and knows why you have brought him out.

Establish a routine and make sure you take your puppy out:

- First thing in the morning
- After mealtimes
- When he wakes up
- After a play session
- Last thing at night

A puppy should be taken out to relieve himself every two hours at an absolute minimum. If you can manage an hourly trip out, so much the better. The more often your puppy gets it right, the quicker he will learn to be clean in the house. It helps if you use a verbal cue, such as "Busy," when your pup is performing and, in time, this will trigger the desired response.

Do not be tempted to put your puppy out on the doorstep in the hope that he will toilet on his own. Most pups simply sit there, waiting to get back inside the house! No matter how bad the weather is, accompany your puppy and give him lots of praise when he per-

forms correctly.

Do not rush back inside as soon as he has finished. Your puppy might start to delay in the hope of prolonging his time outside with you. Praise him, have a quick game, then you can both go inside.

When accidents happen

No matter how vigilant you are, there are bound to be accidents. If you witness the accident, take your puppy outside immediately, and give him lots of praise if he finishes his business out there.

If you are not there when he has an accident, do not scold him when you discover what has happened. He will not remember what he has done and will not understand why you are angry with him. Simply clean it up and resolve to be more vigilant next time.

Make sure you use a deodorizing cleaner made especially for pet urine when you clean up. Otherwise your pup will be drawn to the smell and may be tempted to use the same spot again.

Choosing a diet

There are so many different types of dog food, all claiming to be the best. How do you know what is likely to suit your Dachshund? This is a breed that can easily become overweight, so you need to find a well-balanced diet that is suited to your dog's individual requirements.

You may decide to keep to the diet recommended by your puppy's breeder, and if your pup is thriving there is no need to change.

However, if your puppy is not doing well on the food, or you have problems getting it, you will need to make a change.

When switching diets, it is very important to switch from one food to the other a little at a time, spreading the transition over a week to 10 days. This will avoid the risk of digestive upset.

Dry food

Most dry foods, or kibble, are scientifically formulated to meet all your dog's nutritional needs. Kibble is certainly convenient, and if often less expensive than other diets.

There are many brands of kibble available, and most offer life-stage foods, such as puppy, adult, and senior. There are also special diets for pregnant bitches, working dogs, and prescription diets for weight control, and other health-related conditions.

Which kibble is best? This is a difficult question, and the best plan is to seek advice from your puppy's breeder or your veterinarian.

Kibble can be fed on its own, or along with other types of food. It is best fed in a puzzle toy—a toy dogs must manipulate in some way to get the food out. No dog is too young—or too old!—to start eating kibble from a puzzle toy.

Canned food and pouches

Canned food contains a lot more water than kibble. Some canned foods—although certainly not all—will have fewer carbohydrates than kibble. Read the label carefully so you are aware of the ingre-

dients and, remember, what you put in will affect what comes out.

Canned food can be all or part of your dog's diet. Even if it is only a part, the label should say the diet is complete and balanced for your dog.

Raw and homemade diets

There are some owners who like to prepare meals especially for their dogs—and it is probably much appreciated. The danger is that although the food is tasty, and your Dachshund may appreciate the variety, you cannot be sure that it has the right nutritional balance.

Commercial raw diets may also come fresh or frozen. If you're buying a raw diet, look for a statement on the label that says it's complete and balanced.

If you want to prepare the diet yourself, work with a veterinary nutritionist to formulate a healthy diet for your dog. There are a lot of raw diet recipes on the Internet, but recent research has found that the majority of them do not offer complete and balanced nutrition.

Feeding schedule

When your puppy arrives in his new home, he will need four meals evenly spaced throughout the day. When he is around 12 weeks, you can cut out one of his meals; he may well have started to leave some of his food indicating he is ready to do this. By six months, he can move to two meals a day—a schedule that will suit him for the rest of his life.

Bones and chews

Puppies love to chew, and many adult dogs also enjoy gnawing on a bone. Bones should always be hard and uncooked. Avoid rib bones and poultry bones, as they can splinter and cause major problems. Dental chews, and some of the manufactured rawhide chews, are safe, but they should be given only under supervision.

Ideal weight

The Dachshund may have short legs, but this does not mean his belly should be touching the ground! Dachshund owners seem to struggle more than many to keep their dogs at the correct weight, but it is of vital importance—especially for a breed prone to back problems.

An obese dog may suffer from a number of serious health problems, which can have a major effect on life expectancy. Quality of life will also be affected, as an overweight Dachshund will become progressively less mobile and will not be able to exercise properly.

The Dachshund has perfected the art of looking at you with his dark, melting eyes telling you he is starving. You will therefore need to harden your heart and think of your dog's figure! If you are using treats for training, remember to take these into account and reduce the amount you feed at his next meal.

When you are assessing your dog's weight, look at him from

above, and make sure you can see a definite "waist" behind the ribcage. You should be able to feel his ribs but not see them. When looking at his underside, there should be good ground clearance and a slight tuck-up should be visible when he is viewed from the side.

To keep a close check on your Dachshund's weight, get into the habit of visiting your veterinary clinic monthly so that you can weigh him. Keep a record of his weight so you can make adjustments if necessary.

If you are concerned that your Dachshund is putting on too much weight—or appears to be losing weight—consult your veterinarian, who will give you advice and help you to plan a suitable diet.

Chapter 6

Caring for Your Dachshund

The Dachshund is a relatively easy breed to care for, particularly if you get the right balance between food and exercise so your dog remains fit and active. Make sure you check your dog all over regularly, so you can spot any signs of trouble early on.

Coat Care

This is probably the biggest consideration for a Dachshund. It may take a little time or a lot, depending on the variety you have chosen.

Smooths

This is a very low-maintenance coat, because it doesn't shed much. All a smooth needs is a weekly groom with a hound glove. Some owners prefer to use a soft bristle brush, and either are fine.

If you want to bring out the shine in the coat, you can give your

The smooth Dachshund needs minimal coat care. A quick polish with a bristle brush or hound glove is enough.

The workload steps up with longhairs, who need regular brushing with a slicker brush and combing, with a metal comb. The feathering needs special attention.

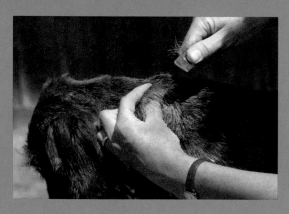

Wirehaired Dachshunds need to be brushed and combed regularly, and have their coats stripped of dead hair at least twice a year.

smooth Dachshund a polish with a chamois cloth. There are a number of lotions on the market that enhance the shine even more, and you can certainly use one if that look appeals to you.

Longhairs

This coat is soft in texture; it may be straight or have a slight wave. To keep it looking its best, regular brushing and combing is needed, as mats and tangles form very easily. Grooming can be a lengthy process if you do not do it at least every other day. Start getting your puppy used to being groomed from an early age, and he will learn to relax and enjoy the procedure.

A bristle brush can be used on the body coat, but a slicker brush is required for the feathering. Work through the feathering, behind the ears where mats form, on the chest, the legs, and the underside. The feathering on the tail will need particular attention. Once you have groomed all the feathering with a slicker brush you need to start again, this time using a wide-toothed metal comb.

Wirehairs

Wirehaired Dachshunds have a double coat, which consists of a dense undercoat and a harsh, wiry topcoat. The topcoat is tight-fitting on the body, with longer hair on the legs, underside, and the facial furnishings, which consist of eyebrows and a beard.

The body coat can be kept neat and healthy with a bristle brush, but the longer hair will need to be combed to prevent matting. Debris, particularly

A Quick Grooming Guide

Use a ball of cotton to clean the inside of the ear flap.

Routine tooth brushing will keep away doggy breath.

Get your Dachshund used to nail trimming from an early age.

food, can collect in the beard, so this must be kept clean and should be combed to prevent mats and tangles.

The wire coat does not shed like other coats. However, it does need to be hand stripped two or three times a year to remove the dead hair. In the show world the process of hand stripping—taking out the dead hair using a stripping knife—is ongoing, gradually working to enhance the dog's shape and outline.

Pet owners generally take their dog to a professional groomer to strip the coat. Clipping is incorrect for wirehaired Dachshunds, as it ruins the harsh texture of the coat.

Some wirehaired Dachshunds are born with a pin wire coat, and this will not need stripping. A typical pin wire has little or no face furnishings, but still has a double coat. The undercoat is dense and the topcoat is harsh, but is generally shorter than the classic wirehaired coat. Pin wire coats can be maintained very easily with a stiff bristle brush.

Bathing

There is no need to regularly bathe your dog, and it's not actually good for her coat. However, Dachshunds do have a tendency to roll, particularly if they can find something especially smelly. If that happens, there is no option but to bathe your dog. Use a

shampoo that is specially formulated for dogs, and rinse thoroughly to make sure no trace remains in the coat.

Routine care

In addition to grooming, you will need to carry out some routine care. Check the eyes for signs of soreness or discharge. You can use a piece of cotton—a separate piece for each eye—and wipe away any debris.

Ears

The ears should be clean and free from odor. You can buy specially manufactured ear wipes, or you can use a piece of cotton to clean the insides of the ear flaps. Do not probe into the ear canal or you risk damaging it.

With longhaired and wirehaired Dachshunds, you may find that hair grows inside the ears and can be a source of problems if it is not removed. This is most easily done using finger and thumb. The pro-

cess is made simpler if you use an ear powder; the hair comes out more easily and causes less distress. Start doing this from an early age, rewarding your puppy for his cooperation, so he learns to accept it without fuss.

Tooth brushing demonstration.

Teeth

Dental disease is becoming more prevalent among dogs, so teeth cleaning should be seen as an essential part of your care regime. The build-up of tartar on the teeth can result in tooth decay, gum infection, and bad breath, and if it is allowed to accumulate, you may have no option but to get your dog's teeth cleaned under anesthesia.

When your Dachshund is still a puppy, accustom him to teeth cleaning so it becomes a matter of routine. Dog toothpaste comes in a variety of meaty flavors, which your Dachshund will like, so you can start by putting some toothpaste on your finger and gently rubbing his teeth. You can then progress to using a finger brush or a toothbrush, whichever you find most convenient.

Remember to reward your Dachshund when he cooperates and then he will positively look forward to his teeth-cleaning sessions.

Feet

Nail trimming is a task dreaded by many dog owners—and many dogs—but, again, if you start early, your Dachshund will get used to the procedure.

Dark nails are harder to trim than white nails because you cannot see the quick (the nerves and veins that run through the nail), which will bleed if it is nicked. The best policy is to trim little and often, so the nails don't grow too long and you do not risk cutting too much and nicking the quick.

If you are worried about trimming your Dachshund's nails, go to your veterinarian so you can see it done properly. If you are still concerned, you can always use the services of a professional groomer.

If you have a longhaired or wirehaired Dachshund, you will also need to inspect the foot pads regularly. Long hair grows between the pads, and this needs to be trimmed. If it is neglected, the hair grows too long and becomes matted, which will be very uncomfortable for your dog.

Exercise

The Dachshund was bred to be a working hound and will need regular, varied exercise. Going for walks gives a dog the opportunity to use her nose and investigate new sights and smells. Dachshunds have an excellent sense of smell, and an opportunity to explore new places will be viewed as a great treat, even if you do not go for miles.

Beware of over-exercising puppies, as this can cause damage, such as out-turned feet, a poor topline, and poor body development. Exercise should be suited to a puppy's age, starting with playing in

the yard or a nearby park, gradually increasing to five-minute walks, 10-minute walks at four months old, 15 to 20 minutes at five months, and 25 to 30 minutes at six months. By the time your Dachshund is 12 months old, she will enjoy walks of around 45 minutes every day.

Back problems

The Dachshund's elongated conformation means there is an increased risk of back problems. Good management will help prevent problems, so all Dachshund owners should:

- Provide regular exercise.
- Prevent your dog from climbing of stairs wherever possible, and make sure she goes slow on staircases.
- Use a ramp when your Dachshund is getting in and out of the car.
- Don't let your Dachshund jump on or off furniture. Offer ramps and doggy steps for getting up and down.
- Always lift a Dachshund using both hands—one to support her chest the other to support her back.

The older Dachshund

We are fortunate the Dachshund has a long life expectancy, and you will not notice any significant changes in your dog until she reaches double figures, or maybe even later.

The older Dachshund will sleep more, and she may be reluctant to go for longer walks. She may show signs of stiffness when she gets up from her bed, but these generally ease when she starts moving. Some older Dachshunds may have impaired vision, and some may become a little deaf, but as long as their senses do not deteriorate dramatically, this is something older dogs learn to live with.

If you treat your older Dachshund with kindness and consideration, she will enjoy her later years and suffer the minimum of discomfort. It is advisable to switch her over to a senior diet, which is more suited to her needs, and you may need to adjust the quantity, as she will not be burning up the calories she did when she was younger and more energetic. Make sure her sleeping quarters are warm and free from drafts, and if she gets wet, make sure you dry her thoroughly.

Most important of all, be guided by your Dachshund. She will have good days when she feels up to going for a walk, and other days when she would prefer to poke around in the yard. If you have a younger dog at home, this may well stimulate your older Dachshund to take more of an interest in what is going on. But make sure she is not pestered, as she needs to rest undisturbed when she is tired.

Letting go

Inevitably there comes a time when your Dachshund is not enjoying a good quality of life, and you need to make the painful decision to let her go. We all wish that our dogs passed, painlessly, in their sleep but, unfortunately, this is rarely the case. However, we can allow our dogs to die with dignity, and to suffer as a little as possible, and this should be our way of saying thank you for the wonderful companionship they have given us.

When you feel the time is drawing close, talk to your veterinarian, who will be able to make an objective assessment of your Dachshund's condition and will help you to make the right decision.

This is the hardest thing you will ever have to do as a dog owner, and it is only natural to grieve for your beloved Dachshund. But eventually, you will be able to look back on the happy memories of times spent together, and this will bring much comfort. You may, in time, feel that your life is not complete without a Dachshund and you will feel ready to welcome a new dog into your home.

Chapter 7

Training Your Dachshund

To live in the modern world without fear and anxieties, and to be welcome wherever he goes, a Dachshund needs socialization and an education in basic manners, so that he learns to cope calmly and confidently in a wide variety of situations.

Early learning

The breeder will have started a program of socialization by getting the puppies used to all the sights and sounds of a busy household. You need to continue this, making sure your pup is not worried by household equipment, such the vacuum cleaner or the washing machine, and that he gets used to noises inside the house and out.

It is also important to handle your puppy all over his body regularly, so he will accept grooming and other routine care, and will not be worried if he has to be examined by the veterinarian.

To begin with, your puppy needs to get used to all the members

of his new family, but then you should give him the opportunity to meet friends and other people who come to the house.

Right from the start, teach him acceptable greeting behavior.

- Have treats ready, and once your puppy has said his first hello, quickly distract his attention by calling him to you, giving him a treat and praising him.
- Let him return to the visitor, and if he is not barking, call him back to you for a treat and praise. In this way, the pup learns that coming to you is more rewarding than barking.
- Now give the visitor a couple of treats so that when your puppy approaches—and is not barking—he can be rewarded.

This training may take a bit of practice, but it is well worth keeping at it. You really don't want your dog barking at everyone he meets.

It is also very important that your puppy learns to interact with children. If you do not have children, make sure your puppy has the chance to meet and play with other people's children, so he learns that humans come in small sizes too.

The outside world

When your puppy has completed his vaccinations, he is ready to venture into the outside world. Dachshund puppies take a lively interest in anything new and will relish the opportunity to broaden their horizons. However, there is a lot for a small puppy to take in, so do not

swamp him with too many new experiences when you first set out.

The best plan is to start in a quiet area with light traffic, and only progress to a busier place when your puppy is ready. There is so much to see and hear—people (maybe carrying bags or umbrellas), wheelchairs, strollers, bicycles, cars, trucks, machinery—so give your puppy a chance to take it all in.

If he does appear worried about anything, do not fall into the trap of sympathizing with him, or worse still, picking him up. This will only teach your pup that he has good reason to be worried and, with luck, you will rescue him if he feels scared.

Instead, give him a little space so he does not have to confront whatever he is frightened of, and distract him with a few treats. Then encourage him to walk past, using a calm, no-nonsense approach. Your pup will take the lead from you and will realize there is nothing to fear.

Your pup also needs to continue his education in canine manners started by his mother and by his littermates, because he needs to be able to greet all dogs calmly, giving the signals that say he is friendly and offers no threat. If you have a friend who has a well-mannered dog, this is an ideal beginning. As your puppy gets older and more established, you can widen his circle of canine acquaintances.

Training classes

A training class will give your Dachshund the opportunity to interact with other dogs, and he will also learn to focus on you in a different, distracting environment. Before you sign up for any class, attend a class as an observer to make sure you are happy with what goes on.

Find out the following:
- How much training experience do the instructors have?
- Are the classes divided into appropriate canine age categories?
- Do the instructors have experience training Dachshunds?
- Do they use positive, reward-based training methods?
- Does the club train for the Canine Good Citizen program?

If the training class is well run, it is certainly worth attending. Both you and your Dachshund will learn useful training exercises. It will increase his social skills, and you will have the chance to talk to lots of like-minded dog enthusiasts.

Training guidelines

The Dachshund is a highly intelligent dog and is generally eager to please. However, he does have a strong will and this can make him stubborn if training becomes monotonous, or if he lacks motivation.

Although you will be eager to get started, do not neglect the fundamentals in training that could make the difference between success and failure. Try to observe the following guidelines:

- Choose an area that is free from distractions so your puppy will focus on you. You can move on to a more challenging environment as your pup progresses.
- Do not train your puppy just after he has eaten or when you have returned from exercise. He will either be too full, or too tired, to concentrate.
- Do not train if you are in a bad mood, or if you are short on time—these sessions always end in disaster!
- Make sure you have a reward your Dachshund values—tasty treats, such as cheese or cooked liver, or an extra-special toy.
- If you are using treats, make sure they are bite-size. Otherwise you will lose momentum when your pup stops to chew his treat.
- Keep your verbal cues simple, and always use the same one for each exercise. For example, when you ask your puppy to go into the Down position, the cue is "Down," not "Lie Down," "Get Down," or anything else. Remember, your dog does not speak English; he simply associates the sound of the

word with the behavior.

- If your Dachshund is finding an exercise difficult, break it down into smaller steps so it is easier to understand.
- Do not make your training sessions boring and repetitious; your dog will quickly lose interest.
- Do not train for too long, particularly with a young puppy who has a very short attention span.
- Always end training sessions on a positive note, with something your puppy can easily get right.
- Above all, have fun, so you and your Dachshund both enjoy spending quality time together.

First lessons

A Dachshund puppy will soak up new experiences like a sponge, so training should start from the time your pup arrives in his new home. It is so much easier to teach good habits rather than trying to correct your puppy when he has established an undesirable pattern of behavior.

Wearing a collar

Your dog should be on a leash when he goes out in public, so he needs to get used to the feel of a collar around his neck. The best plan is to accustom your pup to wearing a soft collar at home for a few minutes at a time, until he gets used to it.

- Fit the collar so that you can get at least two fingers between the collar and his neck. Then have a game to distract his attention. This will work for a few moments; then he will stop, put his back leg up, and scratch away at the peculiar thing around his neck that feels so odd.

- Bend down, rotate the collar, pat him on the head, and distract him by playing with a toy or giving him a treat.
- Gradually increase the time he wears the collar before you take it off him. Once he has worn the collar for a few minutes each day, he will soon ignore it and become used to it.
- Remember, never leave the collar on the puppy unsupervised, especially when he is outside in the yard or when he is in his crate, as it is could get snagged, causing serious injury.

Walking on the leash

- Once your puppy is used to the collar, take him outside into your yard or another securely fenced area where there are no distractions.
- Attach the leash and, to begin with, allow him to wander with the leash trailing, making sure it does not become snagged on anything. Then pick up the leash and follow the pup where he wants to go. He needs to get used to the sensation of being attached to you before you start teaching him to follow.

- The next stage is to get your Dachshund to follow you, and for this you will need some tasty treats. You can show him a treat in your hand and then encourage him to follow you. Walk a few paces, and if he is cooperating, stop and reward him. If he puts on the brakes, simply change direction and lure him with the treat.

- Next, introduce changes of direction so your puppy is walking confidently alongside you. At this stage, introduce a verbal cue, such as "Heel," when your puppy is in the correct position. You can then graduate to walking your puppy outside the fenced area, starting in quiet places and building up to busier environments.

- Do not expect too much of your puppy too soon when you are leash walking away from home. He will be distracted by all the new sights and sounds he encounters, so concentrating on leash training will be difficult for him. Give him a chance to look and see, and reward him frequently when he is walking forward confidently on a loose leash.

Dachshund training

Come when called

Teaching a reliable recall is invaluable for both you and your Dachshund. You are secure in the knowledge that your dog will come back when he is called, and your Dachshund benefits from being allowed off the leash and having the freedom to investigate all the exciting new scents he comes across.

The Dachshund likes to be with his people, but he is a scenthound and the drive to investigate new scents and follow a trail can be overpowering. At these times, a Dachshund will become deaf to your calls, and this can be very frustrating—so much so that you may be reluctant to allow your dog off-leash.

This is counter-productive, because a Dachshund needs the opportunity to exercise, and restricting his freedom will seriously affect his quality of life. You need to work at recalls, providing high-value rewards, so your Dachshund wants to come back to you.

- The breeder may have started this lesson simply by calling the puppies to "Come" at mealtimes, or when they are moving from one place to another.
- You can build on this when your puppy arrives in his new home, calling him to "Come" when he is in a confined space,

such as the kitchen. This is a good place to build up a positive association with the verbal cue—particularly if you ask your puppy to "Come" to get his meals!

- The next stage is to transfer the lesson to the yard or another securely fenced space. Arm yourself with some treats, and wait until your puppy is distracted. Then call him, using a high-pitched, excited tone of voice. At this stage, a puppy wants to be with you, so capitalize on this and keep practicing the verbal cue and rewarding your puppy with a treat and lots of praise when he comes to you.

- Now you are ready to introduce some distractions. Try calling him when someone else is in the yard, or wait a few minutes until he is investigating a really interesting scent. When he responds, make a really big fuss over him and give him extra treats so he knows it is worth his while to come to you.

- If your puppy responds, immediately reward him with a treat. If he is slow to come, run away a few steps and then call again, making yourself sound really exciting. Jump up and down, open your arms wide to welcome him; it doesn't matter how silly you look, he needs to see you as the most fun person in the world.

- When you have a reliable recall around the house and in the yard or some other fenced area, you can venture into the outside world. Do not be too ambitious to begin with; try a recall in a quiet place with a minimum of distractions, and only progress to more challenging environments if your

Dachshund is responding well. Until you are sure he is 100 percent reliable, work on Come with his leash still on.

- Do not make the mistake of only asking your dog to come at the end of a walk. What is the incentive in coming back to you if all you do is clip on his leash and head for home? Instead, call your dog at random times throughout the walk, giving him a treat and a pat, and then letting him go free again. This way, coming to you is always rewarding and does not signal the end of his fun time.

Stationary exercises

The Sit and Down are easy to teach, and mastering these exercises will be rewarding for both you and your Dachshund.

Sit

The best method is to lure your Dachshund into position, and for this you can use a treat, a toy, or his food bowl.

- Hold the reward above his head. As he looks up, he will lower his hindquarters and go into a sit.

- Practice this a few times, and when your puppy understands what you are asking, introduce the verbal cue "Sit."
- When your Dachshund understands the exercise, he will respond to the verbal cue alone, and you will not need to lure and reward him every time he sits. However, you will need to let him know he got it right with praise every time. It is a good idea to give him a treat from time to time when he cooperates, as well, to keep him guessing about when the treats will appear!

Down

This is an important lesson, and can be a lifesaver if an emergency arises and you need to bring your Dachshund to an instant stop.

- You can start with your dog in a Sit for this exercise. Stand or kneel in front of him and show him you have a treat in your hand. Hold the treat just in front of his nose and slowly lower it toward the ground, between his front legs.
- As your Dachshund follows the treat, he will go down on his front legs and, in a few moments, his hindquarters will follow. Close your hand over the treat so he doesn't cheat and get the treat before he is in the correct position. As soon as he is all the way Down, give him the treat and lots of praise.
- Keep practicing, and when your Dachshund understands what you want, introduce the verbal cue "Down."

Control exercises

These exercises can be very useful in a variety of situations. They also get your Dachshund into the habit of cooperating with you, and teach him that when he cooperates, life is very rewarding.

Wait

This exercise teaches your Dachshund to wait in position until you give the next cue. It's a quick behavior, like waiting at the curb until the traffic light changes or waiting in the car until you clip his leash on. It's not the same as Stay, where he must be still for a longer period.

- Start with your puppy on the leash to give you a greater chance of success. Ask him to "Sit" and stand in front him. Step back away one step, holding your hand, palm flat, facing him. Wait a second and then come back to stand in front of him. You can then reward him and release him with a word, such as "Okay."
- Practice this a few times, waiting a little longer before you reward him. When he understands the exercise, introduce the verbal cue "Wait."

- You can reinforce the lesson by using it in different situations, such as asking your Dachshund to "Wait" before you put his food bowl down.

Stay

You need to differentiate this exercise from Wait by using a different hand signal and a different verbal cue.

- Start with your dog in the Down. This position is more comfortable for the long-backed Dachshund, so he is more likely to stay put. Stand at his side and then step forward, with your hand held back, palm facing the dog.
- Step back, release him, and then reward him. Practice until your Dachshund understands the exercise, and then introduce the verbal cue "Stay."
- Gradually increase the distance you can leave your puppy, and increase the challenge by walking around him—and even stepping over him—so that he learns he must stay until you release him. Use the same release word as for Wait.

Leave

A response to this verbal cue means your Dachshund will learn to give up a toy on request, and it follows that he will give up anything when he is asked, which is very useful if he has a forbidden object.

You can also use it if you catch him raiding the trash or digging up a prized plant in the garden.

Some Dachshunds can be a little possessive over toys, and some think that running off with a "trophy" is the greatest fun. This may appear to be harmless, but if your let your Dachshund get away with it, he will think he has the upper hand and may start to take advantage in other situations. It is therefore important to teach your puppy that if he gives up something, he will get a reward that may be even better than the object he had in the first place!

- The "Leave" cue can be taught quite easily when you are first playing with your puppy. As you gently take a toy from his mouth, introduce the verbal cue "Leave," and then praise him.
- If he is reluctant, swap the toy for another toy or a treat. This will usually do the trick.
- Do not try to pull the toy from his mouth if he refuses to give it up, as this will only make him more likely to hang on tight. Let the toy go dead in your hand, and then swap it for a new, exciting toy, so this becomes the better option.
- Remember to make a big fuss over your Dachshund when he cooperates. If he is rewarded with verbal praise, plus a game with a toy or a tasty treat, he will learn that "Leave" is always a good option.

Chapter 8

Keeping Your Dachshund Busy

The Dachshund is a highly intelligent dog, and with positive training she can be welcome everywhere she goes. If you have ambitions to try more advanced training or compete in one of the canine sports, she will be a willing pupil. A few of the most popular canine sports are listed here, but there are many more. The AKC and UKC, and well as the national breed clubs (all listed in Find Out More), are good places to learn about sports for Dachshunds.

Canine Good Citizen

The AKC runs the Canine Good Citizen program. It promotes responsible ownership and helps you to train a well-behaved dog who will fit in with the community. The program tests your dog on basic good manners, alone and with other people and dogs around. It's excellent for all pet owners and is also an ideal starting point if you plan to compete with your dog in any sport.

Obedience

This is a sport where you are assessed as a dog and handler, completing a series of exercises including heel work, recalls, retrieves, stays, send-aways, and scent discrimination. The Dachshund is more than capable of competing in this discipline, but make sure training is fun and you do not put too much pressure on your dog.

The obedience exercises are relatively simple to begin with, involving heel work, a recall, and stays in the lowest classes. As you progress through the levels, more exercises are added, and the aids you are allowed to give are reduced.

To achieve top honors in this discipline requires intensive training, as precision and accuracy are of paramount importance. However, you must guard against drilling your Dachshund, as she will quickly lose motivation.

Agility

It has to be said that the Dachshund does not really have the conformation to compete in agility, but, surprisingly, there are a few who have proved the doubters wrong. Agility is basically a canine obstacle course. In competition, each dog completes the course individually and is assessed on both time and accuracy. The dog who completes the course with the fewest faults, in the fastest time, wins. The obstacles include an A-frame, a dog-walk, weaving poles, a see-saw, tunnels, and jumps.

Rally O

Rally O is loosely based on obedience, and at the highest levels has a few exercises borrowed from agility. Handler and dog must complete a course, in the designated order, that has from 12 to 20 different exercises. The course is timed and the team must complete the course within the limit, but there are no bonus marks for speed.

The great advantage of Rally O is that it is very relaxed, and anyone can compete. In fact, it has proven very popular for handlers with disabilities, as they are able to work their dogs to a high standard and compete on equal terms.

Tracking

The Dachshund is a scenthound, and so tracking is a challenge she thoroughly enjoys. In organized tracking events, dogs must learn to follow scent trails of varying ages, over different types of terrain. These become increasingly tougher as a dog works her way through the levels. The greatest honor is to become a tracking champion.

Dachshund field trials

These AKC field trials are another way to tap into the Dachshund's amazing scenting abilities. A pair of Dachshunds (called a

brace) track a rabbit by its scent trail. The dogs are leashed before they have a chance to catch the rabbit, so no animals are harmed in this sport.

Earthdog and earth work trials

The AKC (earthdog) and UKC (earth work) run trials that are specifically designed to test the working ability of dogs who were bred to "go to ground" (search underground) for quarry. Burrows are located or created, and the dog must work the burrows to find the quarry, which she will indicate by barking, whining, scratching, or digging.

The quarry are protected by wooden bars across the end of the tunnel so they are not endangered. The Dachshund is a highly enthusiastic competitor in this sport and performs with distinction.

Dachshund Club of America Triathlon

In an effort to promote all the qualities of the Dachshund and showcase the versatility of the breed, DCA offers Triathlon awards to Dachshunds who distinguish themselves in performance and companion events. A Dachshund must qualify in three or more of the five event categories (agility, field trial, earthdog, tracking, and obedience/rally), and also pass a conformation evaluation at the national specialty show (a show held annually just for Dachshunds and sponsored by the DCA).

Showing

At a dog show, the judge compares each dog the breed standard, and gives the blue ribbon to the dog who most closely embodies the standard. Exhibiting a dog in the show ring seems easy, but in fact, it requires a lot of training and preparation, particularly when you are asking a strong-minded, working breed to compete in a beauty competition.

If you plan to show your Dachshund, you will need to be a dedicated groomer—or employ the services of a professional—to ensure your dog looks her best when she is examined by the judge.

You will also need to spend time training your Dachshund to perform in the show ring. A dog who does not like being handled by the judge, or one who does not step out boldly on the leash, is never going to win top honors, even if she is a top-quality animal. To do well in the ring, a Dachshund must have that quality that says, "Look at me!"

Chapter 9

Health Care

We are fortunate that the Dachshund is a robust breed and, with good routine care, a well-balanced diet, and sufficient exercise, most will experience few health problems. However, it is your responsibility to put a program of preventive health care in place—and this should start from the moment your puppy, or older dog, arrives in his new home.

Parasites

No matter how well you look after your Dachshund, you will have to accept that parasites—internal and external—are ever present, and you need to take preventive action.

Internal parasites live inside your dog. These are the various worms. Most will find a home in the digestive tract, but there is also a parasite that lives in the heart. If infestation is unchecked, a dog's health will be severely jeopardized, but routine preventive treatment is simple and effective.

External parasites live on your dog's body—in his skin and fur, and sometimes in his ears.

Vaccination Program

The American Animal Hospital Association and the American Veterinary Medical Association have issued vaccination guidelines that apply to all breeds of dogs. They divide the available vaccines into two groups: core vaccines, which every dog should get, and non-core vaccines, which are optional.

Core vaccines are canine parvovirus-2, distemper, and adenovirus-2. Puppies should get vaccinated every three to four weeks between the ages of 6 and 16 weeks, with the final dose at 14 to 16 weeks of age. If a dog older than 16 weeks is getting their first vaccine, one dose is enough. Dogs who received an initial dose at less than 16 weeks should be given a booster after one year, and then every three years or more thereafter.

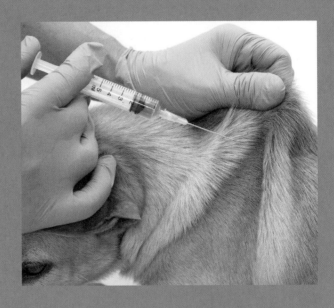

Rabies is also a core vaccine. For puppies less than 16 weeks old, a single dose should be given no earlier than 12 weeks of age. Revaccination is recommended annually or every three years, depending on the vaccine used and state and local laws.

Non-core vaccines are canine parainfluenza virus, Bordetella bronchiseptica, canine influenza virus, canine measles, leptospirosis, and Lyme disease.

The dog's exposure risk, lifestyle, and geographic location all come into play when deciding which non-core vaccines may be appropriate for your dog. Have a conversation with your veterinarian about the right vaccine protocol for your dog.

Roundworm

This is found in the small intestine. Signs of infestation will be a poor coat, a potbelly, diarrhea, and lethargy. Prospective mothers should be treated before mating, but it is almost inevitable that parasites she may have will be passed on to the puppies. For this reason, a breeder will start a worming program, which you will need to continue. Ask your vet for advice on treatment, which will need to continue throughout your dog's life.

Tapeworm

Infection occurs when fleas and lice are ingested; the adult worm takes up residence in the small intestine, releasing mobile segments (which contain eggs) that can be seen in a dog's feces as small rice-like grains. The only other obvious sign of infestation is irritation of the anus. Again, routine preventive treatment is required throughout your Dachshund's life.

Heartworm

This parasite is transmitted by mosquitoes, and is found in all parts of the USA, although its prevalence does vary. Heartworms live in the right side of the heart and larvae can grow up to 14 inches (35 cm) long. A dog with heartworm is at severe risk from heart failure, so preventive treatment, as advised by your vet, is essential. Dogs should also have regular tests to check for the presence of infection.

How to Detect Fleas

You may suspect your dog has fleas, but how can you be sure? There are two methods to try. Run a fine comb through your dog's coat, and see if you can detect the presence of fleas on the skin, or clinging to the comb. Alternatively, sit your dog on some white paper and rub his back. This will dislodge feces from the fleas, which will be visible as small brown specks. To double check, shake the specks on to some damp cotton balls. Flea feces consists of the dried blood taken from the host, so if the specks turn a lighter shade of red, you know your dog has fleas.

Lungworm

Lungworm is a parasite that lives in the heart and major blood vessels supplying the lungs. It can cause many problems, such as breathing difficulties, excessive bleeding, sickness, diarrhea, seizures, and even death. The dog becomes infected when ingesting slugs and snails, often accidentally when rummaging through undergrowth. Lungworm is not common, but it is on the increase and a responsible owner should be aware of it. Fortunately, it is easily preventable, and even affected dogs usually make a full recovery if treated early enough. Your vet will be able to advise you on the risks in your area and what form of treatment may be required.

Fleas

A dog may carry many types of fleas. The flea stays on the dog only long enough to feed and breed, but its presence will cause itching. If your dog is allergic to fleas—usually a reaction to the flea's saliva—he will scratch himself until he is raw. Spot-ons and chewable flea preventives are easy to use and highly effective, and should be given regularly to prevent fleas entirely. Some also prevent ticks.

If your dog has fleas, talk to your veterinarian about the best treatment. Bear in mind that your entire home, dog's whole environment, and all other pets in your home will also need to be treated.

Ticks

These are blood-sucking parasites that are most frequently found in areas where sheep or deer are present.

The main danger is their ability to pass a wide variety of very serious diseases—including Lyme disease—to both dogs and humans. The preventive you give your dog for fleas generally works for ticks, but you should discuss the best product to use with your veterinarian.

Ear mites

These parasites live in the outer ear canal. The signs of infestation are a brown, waxy discharge, and your dog will often shake his head and scratch his ear. If you suspect your dog has ear mites, a visit to the vet will be needed so that medicated ear drops can be prescribed.

Cheyletiella mange

These small, white mites are visible to the naked eye and are often referred to as "walking dandruff." They cause a scruffy coat and mild itchiness. They are zoonotic—transferable to humans—so prompt treatment with an insecticide prescribed by your veterinarian is essential.

Chiggers

These are picked up from the undergrowth, and can be seen as bright red, yellow, or orange specks on the webbing between the toes, although this can also be found elsewhere on the body, such as on the ear flaps. Treatment is effective with the appropriate insecticide, prescribed by your vet.

Skin mites

There are two types of parasite that burrow into a dog's skin. Demodex canis is transferred from a mother to her pups while they are feeding. Treatment is with a topical preparation, and sometimes antibiotics are needed. Refer to your vet.

The other skin mite is sarcoptes scabiei, which causes intense itching and hair loss. It is highly contagious, so all dogs in a household will need to be treated, which involves repeated bathing with a medicated shampoo.

Common ailments

As with all living animals, dogs can be affected by a variety of ailments, most of which can be treated effectively after consulting with your vet, who will prescribe appropriate medication and will advise you on how to care for your dog's needs.

Here are some of the more common problems that could affect your Dachshund, with advice on how to deal with them.

Anal glands

These are two small sacs on either side of the anus, which produce a dark brown secretion. The anal glands should empty every

How to Remove a Tick

If you spot a tick on your dog, do not try to pick it off, as you risk leaving the hard mouth parts embedded in his skin. The best way to remove a tick is to use a fine pair of tweezers, or you can buy a tick remover. Grasp the tick head firmly and then pull the tick straight out from the skin. If you are using a tick remover, check the instructions, as some recommend a circular twist when pulling. When you have removed the tick, clean the area with mild soap and water.

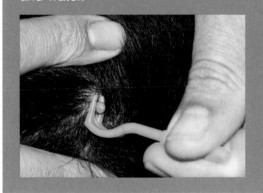

time a dog defecates, but if they become blocked or impacted, a dog will experience increasing discomfort. He may lick at his rear end, or scoot his bottom along the ground to relieve the irritation.

Treatment involves a trip to the vet, who will empty the glands manually. It is important to do this without delay or they could become infected.

Dental problems

Vets report that dental problems are becoming increasingly common among dogs, and can cause serious discomfort. Good dental hygiene will do much to minimize problems with gum infection and tooth decay. If tartar accumulates to the extent that you cannot remove it by brushing, your dog will need to be anesthetized for a dental cleaning by the veterinarian.

Diarrhea

There are many reasons why a dog has diarrhea, but most commonly it is the result of scavenging, a sudden change of diet, or an adverse reaction to a particular type of food.

If your dog is suffering from diarrhea, the first step is to withhold food for a day. It is important that he does not become dehydrated, so make sure fresh drinking water is available. However, drinking too much can increase the diarrhea, which may be accompanied with vomiting, so limit how much he drinks at any one time.

After allowing the stomach to

rest, feed a bland diet, such as white fish or chicken with boiled rice for a few days. In most cases, your dog's motions will return to normal and you can resume normal feeding, although this should be done gradually.

A vet shows how to clean ears.

However, if this fails to work and the diarrhea persists for more than a few days, you should consult your vet. Your dog may have an infection, which needs to be treated with antibiotics, or the diarrhea may indicate some other problem that needs expert diagnosis.

Ear infections

The Dachshund has drop ears that lie close to his head. This means that air cannot circulate as freely as it would in a dog whose ears stand up. Therefore, it is important to check them regularly.

A healthy ear is clean, with no sign of redness or inflammation, and no evidence of a waxy brown discharge or a foul odor. If you see your dog scratching her ear, shaking her head, or holding one ear at an odd angle, you will need to consult your vet. The most likely causes are ear mites, an infection, or there may be a foreign body, such as a grass seed, trapped in the ear.

Depending on the cause, treatment is with medicated ear drops, possibly containing antibiotics. If a foreign body is suspected, the vet will need to carry out further investigation.

Eye problems

The Dachshund has medium eyes, set obliquely in the skull. They do not protrude—which is important, as breeds with prominent eyes, such as the Pekingese, are vulnerable to injury.

If your Dachshund's eyes look red and sore, he may be suffering from conjunctivitis. This may, or may not be accompanied with a watery or a crusty discharge. Conjunctivitis can be caused by a bacterial or viral infection, it could be the result of an injury, or it could be an adverse reaction to pollen.

You will need to consult your vet for a correct diagnosis, but in the case of an infection, treatment with medicated eye drops is effective. Conjunctivitis may also be the first sign of more serious inherited eye problems, which will be discussed later in this chapter. Some dog mays suffer from dry, itchy eyes, which they may make worse by scratching. This condition, keratoconjunctivitis sicca, may be inherited.

Foreign bodies

In the home, puppies—and some older dogs—cannot resist chewing anything that looks interesting. The toys you choose for your dog should be suitably robust to withstand damage, but children's toys can be irresistible. Some dogs will chew—and swallow—anything from socks, underwear, and any other items from the laundry basket to golf balls and stones from the garden. Obviously, these items are indigestible and could cause an obstruction in your dog's intestine, which is potentially lethal.

The signs to look for are vomiting and a tucked-up posture. The dog will often be restless and will look as if he is in pain. In this situation, you must get your dog to the vet without delay, as surgery will be needed to remove the obstruction.

Heatstroke

The Dachshund has a long muzzle and an unobstructed respiratory system. This means he does not suffer from the breathing problems of flat-nosed breeds, such as Pugs and Bulldogs. However, all dogs can overheat on hot days, and this can have disastrous consequences.

If the weather is warm, make sure your Dachshund always has access to shady areas, and wait for a cooler part of the day before going for a walk. Never leave your dog in the car, as the temperature

can rise dramatically—even on a cloudy day. Heatstroke can happen very rapidly, and unless you are able lower your dog's temperature, it can be fatal.

The signs of heatstroke include heavy panting and difficulty breathing, bright red tongue and mucous membranes, thick saliva, and vomiting. Eventually, the dog becomes progressively unsteady and passes out.

If your dog appears to be suffering from heatstroke, this is a true emergency. Lie him flat and then cool him as quickly as possible by hosing him down or covering him with wet towels. As soon as he has made some recovery, take him to the vet.

Lameness or limping

There are a wide variety of reasons why a dog might go lame, from a simple muscle strain to a fracture, ligament damage, or more complex problems with the joints, including inherited disorders. The Dachshund's elongated back means that spinal problems may occur. You need to be extra vigilant, making sure your Dachshund is moving freely, and avoiding exercise that could put an undue strain on his back. It takes an expert to make a correct diagnosis, so if you are concerned about your dog, do not delay in seeking help.

In general, don't encourage a lot of jumping (into the car, for example, or on and off furniture) as this causes shock on the disks of the spine. When lifting and carrying your dog, support his weight both front and rear, so his spine is not stressed.

As your Dachshund gets older, he may suffer from arthritis, which you will see as general stiffness, particularly when he gets up after resting. It will help if you ensure his bed is in a warm draft-free location, and if your Dachshund gets wet after exercise, you must dry him thoroughly. If your Dachshund seems to be in pain, consult your vet, who will be able to help with pain relief medication and nutritional supplements.

Skin problems

If your dog is scratching or nibbling at his skin, first check that he is free from fleas. There are other external parasites that cause itching and hair loss, but you will need a vet to help you find the culprit.

An allergic reaction is another major cause of skin problems. It can be quite an undertaking to find the cause of the allergy, and you will need to follow your vet's advice, which often requires eliminating specific ingredients from the diet, as well as looking at environmental factors.

Inherited disorders

Like all breeds, the Dachshund does have a few inherited disorders that tend to run in the breed. If your dog is diagnosed with any of the diseases listed here, it is important to remember that they can affect offspring, so it is not wise to breed affected dogs.

There are now recognized screening tests that enable breeders to check for carrier and affected individuals, and hence reduce the prevalence of these diseases within the breed. DNA testing is also becoming more widely available, and as research into genetic diseases progresses, more DNA tests are being developed.

Endocrine disorders

Hypothyroidism, or impaired thyroid gland function with low thyroid hormone levels, is seen in Dachshunds. It often develops slowly over several months or years. The dog may be listless, with a poor coat, and often gains weight. This disease is not easy to diagnose, and repeated testing may be necessary. It is treated with thyroid supplements.

Cushing's disease is caused by an excess of corticosteroid hormones, and occurs most often in older dogs. Signs include weight gain, increased thirst, and increased urine output. Medical treatments are available.

Diabetes is a metabolic disorder of the pancreas that results in an impaired ability to metabolize glucose. The first signs are often increased thirst and increased urine output. There are a number of treatments available, depending on the severity of the disease.

Eye disorders

The Canine Eye Registration Foundation (CERF) was set up by dog breeders concerned about inheritable eye disease, and provides a database of dogs who have been examined by diplomates of the American College of Veterinary Ophthalmologists. You should ask to see CERF testing results of the parents of any puppy you are considering.

Distichiasis is seen most often in miniature longhaired Dachshunds. There is an extra row of eyelashes, which rub on the cornea. Surgery is required in severe cases.

Entropion is a condition in which the eyelid turns inward,

scratching the cornea or conjunctiva. If untreated, it can cause permanent damage and blindness. It is extremely painful and is easily detected, because the dog will blink excessively and his eyes will be watery. Surgery is reasonably straightforward and effective. Affected dogs should not be bred.

Progressive retinal atrophy is a bilateral degenerative disease of the cells (rods and cones) of the retina, leading initially to night blindness and progressing to complete loss of vision. Dogs are affected from three to four years of age, and there is no cure. There is a test available for younger dogs, to prevent carriers from passing on the genetic defect.

Optic nerve hypoplasia is more often seen in miniature longhaired Dachshunds. The optic nerve fails to develop, resulting in blindness. Tests are available.

Cataracts cloud the lens of your dog's eyes. They can appear in either or both eyes. Some cataracts are small and do not grow, some grow slowly, but others can render your dog blind in a short time.

Skeletal problems

Intervertebral disc disease (IVDD) affects the discs between the vertebra. In a puppy born with the disease, the degeneration of these discs begins to occur within the first few months. As the discs degenerate over time, they become less able to withstand compression. If too much force is placed on them, they can be squeezed and expand or rupture. Typically this happens without warning at around three to six years of age. The ruptured disc extrudes into the spinal canal, where the spinal cord is.

IVDD is highly suspected to be a hereditary disease in dogs with dwarfed legs, and by some estimates, 20 percent of all Dachshunds

have it to some extent. The signs include lethargy, stiff or hunched back, sensitivity when touched, shivering or shaking, hind limb weakness, poor appetite, or loss of bladder and bowel control. If left untreated, permanent paralysis may occur. IVDD is therefore a true emergency.

Depending on the severity of the damage to the discs, strict crate rest, medical management, and acupuncture may be the first option. Surgical treatment is often successful, but some dogs are permanently handicapped.

In a dog with **patellar luxation**, the kneecap slips out of place because of anatomical deformities in the joint. Dachshunds are not genetically prone to this condition, but because of their short legs, which changes the angle of the kneecap, they are more likely to develop it. Treatment involves rest and anti-inflammatory medications. In more severe cases, surgery may be the best option.

Color dilution alopecia

This is a condition in which dogs develop a gradual thinning of hair on their bodies, often progressing to widespread permanent hair loss. This condition develops in some, but not all dogs that have been bred for dilute coat colors, such as fawn (a dilution of the red or brown coat) and blue (a dilution of the normal black and tan coat).

It is an inherited condition, although the coat will appear normal at birth. Most affected dogs will show signs between six months and as three years of age. Affected dogs can lead a normal life with a little extra care of the skin and perhaps a sweater in the cold.

Lafora disease

This occurs in miniature wirehaired Dachshunds; onset is from five years onwards. It is a form of epilepsy caused by a specific gene mutation. A DNA test is now available.

Mitral valve disease

This is a heart condition in which blood leaking through the mitral valve can be heard as a murmur when a dog is examined with a stethoscope. Signs include intolerance to exercise, coughing, and breathlessness. In severe cases, heart failure may result. Treatment will depend on the severity of the case.

Summing up

This has been a long list of health problems, but it was not my intention to scare you. Acquiring some basic knowledge is an asset, as it will allow you to spot signs of trouble at an early stage. Early diagnosis very often leads to the most effective treatment.

The Dachshund as a breed is a generally healthy, energetic dog with a zest for life, and annual check-ups will be all he needs. As a companion, he will bring many happy memories in the years you will spend together.

Find Out More

Books

Bradshaw, John. *Dog Sense: How the New Science of Dog Behavior Can Make You a Better Friend to Your Pet.* New York: Basic Books, 2014.

Eldredge, Debra, DVM, and Kate Eldredge, *Idiot's Guides: Dog Tricks.* New York: Alpha, 2015.

Eldredge, Debra M., DVM, Liisa D. Carlson, DVM, Delbert G. Carlson, DVM, and James M. Giffin, MD. *Dog Owner's Home Veterinary Handbook*, 4th Ed.. New York: Howell Book House, 2007.

Frier-Murza, Jo Ann, *Earthdog Ins and Outs: Guiding Natural Instincts for Success in Earthdog Tests and Den Trials*, 2nd Ed., VGF Publications, 2010.

Stilwell, Victoria. *Train Your Dog Positively: Understand Your Dog and Solve Common Behavior Problems Including Separation Anxiety, Excessive Barking, Aggression, Housetraining, Leash Pulling, and More!.* Berkeley: Ten Speed Press, 2013.

Websites

www.akc.org American Kennel Club

www.dachshundclubofamerica.org Dachshund Club of America

dachshund-nmdc.org National Miniature Daschund Club

www.petmd.com PetMD

www.ukcdogs.com United Kennel Club

agility   in this case, a canine sport in which dogs navigate an obstacle course

breed standard   a detailed written description of the ideal type, size, shape, colors, movement, and temperament of a dog breed

conforms   aligns with, agrees with

docked   cut or shortened

dysplasia   a structural problem with the joints, when the bones do not fit properly together

heatstroke   a medical condition in which the body overheats to a dangerous degree

muzzle   (n) the nose and mouth of a dog; (v) to place a restraint on the mouth of a dog

neuter   to make a male dog unable to create puppies

parasites   organisms that live and feed on a host organism

pedigree   the formal record of an animal's descent, usually showing it to be purebred

socialization   the process of introducing a dog to as many different sights, sounds, animals, people and experiences as possible, so he will feel comfortable with them all

spay   to make a female dog unable to create puppies

temperament   the basic nature of an animal, especially as it affects their behavior

Index

adult dogs, 39
agility sports, 105
alopecia, 125
anal glands, 115-116
bathing, 79-80
beds, 55-56
body, 21 fig, 23
bones and chews, 72
bowls, 57
breed development, 15-17
breed standards
    forequarters, 23, 25
    gait, movement, 28
    head, skull, 21-22
    hindquarters, feet, 25
    mouth, neck, 23
    purpose of, 18, 20
breeders, 43-45
Canine Good Citizen, 102
chiggers, 114
coat colors, 24, 35
coat types, 9, 25-27
collars, 56, 92-93
commitment, 32-34
companion dogs, 11, 28, 30-31
companion puppies, 48
control exercises, 99-101
crates, 55
Cushing's disease, 121
Dachshund Club of America, 107
Dachshund field trials, 105-106
Dachshunds
    adopting multiple, 37-39
    popularity of, 17
    roles of, 6
    standard sizes of, 27
dental care, 81, 116
diabetes, 121
diarrhea, 116-117
diets, 70-71
disorders, 121
distichiasis, 122
ears
    cleaning, 80-81

size and shape of, 22-23
    treating infections in, 117
    treating mites in, 113
earthdog/earth work trials, 106
entropion, 122-123
exercise, 33, 82-83
eyes
    common problems of, 117-118
    disorders of, 122
    size and color of, 22
family and children, 61-62
family pets, 63-65
feeding schedules, 72
female dogs, 35-37
fleas, 112-113
food
    puppy, 57-58, 65
    types of, 70-71
grooming, 74, 76-79
grooming equipment, 58
health issues, 46-47, 83
heatstroke, 118-119
home safety, 50, 52
house rules, 53-54
housetraining, 67-69
hypothyroidism, 121
identification, 56-57
intervertebral disc disease, 123-124
lafora disease, 125
lameness/limping, 119-120
leashes, 56-57, 93-95
life expectancy, 11
longhairs
    grooming, 77
    history of, 17
    ideal coat of, 26-27
male dogs, 35-37
mange, 114
mental stimulation, 33-34
mitral valve disease, 125
nail trimming, 81-82
obedience sports, 104
old dogs, 83-85

origins, 12-13, 15
parasites, 108
physical characteristics, 8-9
puppies
    finding, 40, 42-43
    first night with, 65-67
    questions regarding, 45-46
    settling in, 60-61
    watching, 47-48
Rally O, 105
rescued dogs, 37
scenthounds, 9
show dogs, 31, 49
showing, 107
skin mites, 115
skin problems, 120
sleeping arrangements, 65-67
smooth haired
    development of, 16
    grooming, 74, 76-77
    ideal coat of, 26
socializing, 86, 88-89
sporting dogs, 32
stationary exercises, 97-99
temperament, 9-11, 20-21
ticks, 113-115
toys, 58-59
tracking events, 105
training
    classes for, 90
    collar, 92-93
    come when called, 95-97
    do's and don'ts of, 91-92
    leash, 92, 94-95
vaccines, 110
veterinarians, 59-60
weight, 73
wirehairs
    grooming, 77, 79
    history of, 16
    ideal coat of, 26
    working dogs, 32
    worms, 111-112
yard safety, 52-53